WORDLY WISE 3000®

THIRD EDITION

BOOK 9

Systematic Academic Vocabulary Development

Kenneth Hodkinson | Sandra Adams

EDUCATORS PUBLISHING SERVICE
Cambridge and Toronto

Editorial Project Manager: Kate Moltz
Senior Editor: Will Tripp
Editor: Rachel Smith
Senior Designer: Deborah Rodman
Cover Design: Michelle Mohnkern

Printed in Benton Harbor, MI, in August 2021
ISBN 978-0-8388-7609-1

12 PPG 22 21

Contents

Welcome to *Wordly Wise 3000*®

You've been learning words all your life. At first, you learned them only by hearing other people talk. As you became a reader, you acquired another way to learn words, and you're still learning them.

Obviously, it's important to know what words mean. Your studies so far in school have proven that time and time again. We might be tempted to skip words we don't know—particularly difficult words—when we see them in textbooks. But this affects how well we understand what we read. And after all, the goal of all reading—whether in books we read for pleasure, textbooks, or online—is comprehension. Read this sentence from a job application:

> *All applicants are required to have an up-to-date* catalipan *if they wish to be considered for the position.*

You can probably read and understand every word in the sentence except *catalipan*, because it's a nonsense word. You might say, "Well, it's only one word." But if it were a real word, you would have no idea of what up-to-date item you need. This would not be a good idea if you were applying for the job.

Clearly, the more words you know, the better your understanding of everything you read. *Wordly Wise 3000* will help you learn many words, but it can't teach you *all* the words you'll ever need. It can, however, help guide your learning of new words on your own.

How Do You Learn Word Meanings?

There are two main ways you learn what words mean: indirectly and directly.

You learn word meanings *indirectly* by hearing and reading the words. In fact, the more you listen and read, the more words you'll learn. Reading books, magazines, and online can help build your vocabulary.

But you also have to learn some words *directly*. You may study them for a class, look them up in a dictionary or glossary, or ask someone what they mean. At school, you learn a lot of words directly.

Since you are using this book, you are learning words directly. You are reading the words, learning what they mean, and studying them. Then you are practicing them as you do the activities. Finally, you might even use them in your own writing or conversations. There is an old saying: "Use a word three times and it's yours." Three times might not be enough, of course, but the idea is right. The more you practice using a word, the better you understand it.

What Is "School Language"?

School language refers to the vocabulary you find in the books you read, from novels to textbooks, and on tests. You read them online as you look up information. Your teacher uses these words to explain a math or reading concept. Some have to do with a particular topic, such as the Hubble Telescope, for example. Others are important academic terms, such as *hypothesis*. No matter how much you talk casually with friends and watch television or movies, you will not hear enough of this type of school language to learn the words you need to know. That's why you often need to study such words directly.

Wordly Wise 3000 is designed to teach you some of these words you need to do well in school. Many of the words in *Wordly Wise 3000* are those you will find on college entrance tests, such as the SAT and ACT, on state tests, and on tests required for high school graduation. *Wordly Wise 3000* will also help you learn how to learn more words. Remember, there is no single thing that will help you comprehend what you read as much as knowing word meanings will.

How Do You Figure Out Word Meanings?

What should you do when you come to a word and you think you don't know what it means?

Say It
First, say it to yourself. Maybe once you do this, it will sound like a word you *do* know. Sometimes you know a word in your head without knowing what it looks like in print. So if you match up what you know and what you read—you have the word!

Use Context

If this doesn't work, take the next step: look at the context of the word—the other words and sentences around it. Sometimes these can give you a clue to the word's meaning. Here's an example:

> *Will and Karen spent the night dealing with the* odoriferous *creature.*

Say that you don't know what *odoriferous* means. What kind of creature did Will and Karen have to deal with? A monster? An insect? Then you read on:

> *Their dog, Dickens, had been sprayed by a skunk as he went out for his nighttime walk. They spent the next hour bathing the poor animal in tomato juice to get ride of the smell.*

Now you see that the *odoriferous* creature is a dog that has been sprayed by a skunk—as you know, an animal that sprays a terrible-smelling substance when frightened. You reread the sentence using that meaning. Yes, that works. In this sentence, *odoriferous* means "giving off a foul odor."

Use Word Parts

If the context doesn't help, look at the parts of the word. Does it have any prefixes you know? How about suffixes? Or roots? These can help you figure out what it means. Read this sentence:

> *Kareem Abdul Jabbar was* inducted *into the Basketball Hall of Fame in 1995.*

If you don't know the meaning of *inducted*, try looking at parts of the word. *In-* is a prefix that means "in" or "into." The root *duc* or *duct* comes from the Latin word *ducere*, meaning "to lead." Finally, you know that the *-ed* suffix indicates that the word is in the past tense. So you put it together and figure out that *inducted* means "led or brought into." That makes perfect sense in this sentence.

Look It Up

If saying the word or using context and word parts don't work, you can look it up in a dictionary—either a book or online reference—or a glossary.

Nobody knows the meaning of every word, but good readers know how to use these strategies to figure out words they don't know. Get into the habit of using them as you read, and you may be surprised at how automatic it becomes.

How Well Do You Know a Word?

It's important to know many words and to keep on learning more. But it's also important to know them well. In fact, some experts say that there are four levels of knowing a word:

1. I never saw/heard it before.
2. I've heard/seen it, but I don't know what it means.
3. I think it has something to do with…
4. I know it.*

Just because you can read a word and have memorized its definition, it doesn't mean that you know that word well, or deeply. You want to know it so well that you know when to use it and when to use another word instead. One way to help deepen your knowledge of a word is to use a graphic organizer like the one below that tells about the word *promontory*.

Concept of Definition Map

What is this?
a high point of land that juts
out into the water

Examples
cape, headland,
peninsula

Non-examples
island, hill,
continent

promontory

What is it like?
might be made of rock
is attached to larger land mass

If you can fill in all the parts of this graphic organizer, you are well on your way to really knowing the word *promontory*.

*Dale, E., & O'Rourke, J. (1986). *Vocabulary Building*. Columbus, OH: Zaner-Bloser.

Free Website: WordlyWise3000.com

Did you know you can access *Wordly Wise 3000* online?

Go to www.WordlyWise3000.com and you will find:

Word Lists for all the lessons

The Word Lists allow you to read the words and their definitions and listen to how they are pronounced.

The Word Lists can also be downloaded onto your MP3 player. You can download them and study them wherever you are— home, on the bus, in study period—a great use of your time.

A Quick Check question for every word

You can check your understanding of each word right away. That helps you know which words you need to spend more time studying.

Games and crossword puzzles for every book

Some of them are grouped to use as reviews, just as you would use the Review Puzzles in your book. Use them to practice and have fun with the words you've learned.

Good luck in your study of words. It takes some work, but it will pay off in the end.

For more practice and games, go to **www.WordlyWise3000.com**.

Word List

Study the definitions of the words. Then do the exercises that follow.

bewail
bē wāl'

v. To express deep regret or sorrow over.
Many football fans **bewailed** the replacement of real grass by AstroTurf when the new stadium was built.

destitute
des'tə tōot

adj. 1. Without resources or possessions, especially the necessities of life.
Winter is especially painful for **destitute** people in the cities of the Northeast.

2. Lacking; devoid of.
Staring at the blank sheet of paper on which I was supposed to write a poem, I found myself **destitute** of ideas.

destitution *n.*
Destitution caused by the mid-nineteenth-century potato famine forced many Irish families to seek better lives in the United States.

detract
dē trakt'

v. To take away, especially from the value, beauty, or importance of.
The addition of a modern family room **detracted** from the cozy style of the bungalow.

detractor *n.*
The plan's **detractors** were especially critical of the expected cost of the new town hall.

emancipate
ē man'sə pāt

v. To set free from slavery; to liberate.
Some teenagers feel **emancipated** when they get a driver's license.

emancipation *n.*
In 1863, Abraham Lincoln's **Emancipation** Proclamation stated that all slaves in the Confederacy were, from then on, free.

extol
ek stōl'

v. To praise highly.
The scout leader **extolled** the virtues of truth and honor.

flamboyant
flam boi'ənt

adj. Excessively showy; unrestrained.
My conservative aunt considered her husband's brightly colored, boldly patterned necktie too **flamboyant** for the governor's reception.

flamboyance or **flamboyancy** *n.*
With an air of **flamboyance,** the actor flung out her arm and pointed to the door.

impetus
im'pə təs

n. 1. A driving force; anything that causes an action.
Her hope of winning an athletic scholarship provided the **impetus** for years of grueling training on the swim team.

2. Increased activity resulting from a driving force.
The drop in interest rates gave **impetus** to the real estate market after last year's slump in sales.

insuperable in soo′pər ə bəl	*adj.* Incapable of being overcome or defeated. During my senior year, passing Greek seemed an **insuperable** obstacle to my graduating with my class.
intermittent in tər mit′nt	*adj.* Not continuous; happening at intervals. Showers were **intermittent** throughout the day, although the forecast had promised sunshine.
maxim maks′im	*n.* A general truth or rule of conduct; a short saying. Remember the **maxim** "Haste makes waste" and slow down!
obligatory ə blig′ə tôr ē	*adj.* Required or demanded. Physical education is **obligatory** unless you have a medical excuse for skipping gym class.
plumb plum	*v.* 1. To measure the depth of water. The lake was too deep for us to **plumb.** 2. To reach the deepest part of. The bathyscaphe is a vessel designed to **plumb** the oceans of the world. 3. To understand by examining closely; to solve. Her latest book of poems is a valiant attempt to **plumb** the human soul. *adj.* Straight up and down; vertical. The bricklayer keeps checking to make sure that the wall being built is **plumb.**
vagabond vag′ə bänd	*n.* A person who wanders from place to place. He spent a few years as a **vagabond** before settling in a city and getting a job in a factory. *adj.* The **vagabond** life of traveling musicians suited the members of the band.
visage viz′ij	*n.* A face, especially one that expresses feelings. The smiling **visage** of a young girl looked out from the portrait.
wheedle hwēd′əl	*v.* 1. To coax by using sly persuasion or insincere praise. He tried to **wheedle** his father into lending him the new sports car. 2. To gain by using sly persuasion or insincere praise. The agent **wheedled** several thousand dollars from the couple for a life insurance policy that was practically worthless.

Read the sentences. If a sentence correctly uses the word in bold, write _C_ on the line. If a sentence is incorrect, rewrite it so that the vocabulary word in bold is used correctly.

1. To **emancipate** someone is to release that person.

   _____

   _____

2. An **obligatory** assignment is one that causes great hardship.

   _____

   _____

3. An **impetus** sets something into action.

   _____

   _____

4. To **plumb** a mystery is to understand it by thinking about it carefully.

   _____

   _____

5. A **vagabond** is a person who lacks the necessities of life.

   _____

   _____

6. To **wheedle** something from someone is to obtain it by cajoling that person into giving it.

   _____

   _____

7. To **extol** someone is to show very high regard for that person.

   _____

   _____

8. An **intermittent** noise is one that keeps stopping and starting.

   _____

   _____

9. A person's **visage** is that person's feelings about herself.

   _____

   _____

10. **Destitution** is the state of having all that one could ask for.

    _____

    _____

11. To **bewail** something is to complain about it.

_____

_____

12. A **detractor** is someone to whom another person is attracted.

_____

_____

13. If something is **insuperable,** its parts cannot be separated from the whole.

_____

_____

14. A **maxim** is the larger of two amounts.

_____

_____

15. **Flamboyance** is lack of restraint in one's dress or behavior.

_____

_____

| 1B | Using Words |

If the word (or a form of the word) in bold fits in a sentence in the group following it, write the word in the blank space. If the word does not fit, leave the space empty. There may be more than one correct answer.

bewail

destitute

detract

emancipate

extol

flamboyant

impetus

insuperable

intermittent

maxim

obligatory

plumb

vagabond

visage

wheedle

1. **vagabond**

   (a) As actors in a traveling company, we led a _____ life.

   (b) A true _____ becomes restless after two weeks in one place.

   (c) I cashed in my _____ when I ran short of money.

2. **bewail**

   (a) When he cannot see Juliet, Romeo _____ his fate.

   (b) We must _____ them to try harder next time.

   (c) Did you _____ them of the news that we close permanently tomorrow?

3. **intermittent**

   (a) The _____ traffic noises from the city streets below disturbed my sleep.

   (b) The daily paper made _____ appearances on the newsstands.

   (c) What is the cause of these _____ oil leaks from the engine?

4. **extol**

   (a) She loves to _____ the virtues of small-town America.

   (b) The kidnappers attempted to _____ a million dollars from the wealthy family.

   (c) I will continue to _____ her to practice the piano.

5. **plumb**

   (a) Even Sherlock Holmes could not _____ this mystery.

   (b) When we built the house, we hired an electrician to _____ the house.

   (c) If the walls are not _____, the doors will not hang properly.

6. **destitute**

   (a) We had to admit that we were _____ of fresh ideas.

   (b) The mayor's council is making plans to help the city's _____ people.

   (c) The house is completely _____ and needs to be torn down.

7. **obligatory**

   (a) It is not _____ to have someone accompany you.

   (b) It is _____ to carry your driver's license when driving.

   (c) Stopping at a red light is _____ in all fifty states.

8. **emancipate**

   (a) The recipe instructed cooks to _____ the cream before adding it to the melted chocolate.

   (b) I managed to _____ a hundred dollars from my uncle.

   (c) The candidate was unable to _____ more than fifty votes.

1C Word Study

Each group of words contains two words that are either synonyms or antonyms. Circle them. Then circle _S_ if they are synonyms or _A_ if they are antonyms.

1. bewail	admit	pretend	celebrate	S	A
2. precise	secret	wealthy	destitute	S	A
3. estimate	detract	obtain	enhance	S	A
4. enslave	provide	assist	emancipate	S	A

5. extol	wheedle	praise	pause	S	A
6. towering	active	shy	flamboyant	S	A
7. coax	reward	wheedle	recover	S	A
8. impetus	face	visage	payment	S	A
9. heavy	deep	plumb	vertical	S	A
10. smart	strict	voluntary	obligatory	S	A

 1D   Images of Words

Circle the letter of each sentence that suggests the numbered bold vocabulary word. In each group, you may circle more than one letter or none at all.

1. **wheedle**
   (a) Fido stands by the door when he wants to be taken for a walk.
   (b) If you don't help me, I'll tell Mom who broke the window.
   (c) C'mon. You're my favorite aunt; please lend me the money!

2. **destitution**
   (a) Because of the financial catastrophe, the family had to rely temporarily on welfare benefits from the government.
   (b) The pain is in my lower back, doctor.
   (c) I can't believe you spent fifty dollars on comic books!

3. **impetus**
   (a) On the spur of the moment, I decided to join my sister in Maine.
   (b) I began to take music lessons after inheriting my grandfather's violin.
   (c) I worked all night in order to meet the nine o'clock deadline.

4. **extol**
   (a) Ah! There's nothing like fall in New England!
   (b) Maintaining a good diet and getting more exercise has made me feel really good.
   (c) The Rangers are formidable rivals this season.

5. **detract**
   (a) My father said I'd be doing myself a favor if I shaved off my beard.
   (b) He looked very well-groomed except for his muddy shoes.
   (c) I apologized for expressing my impatience with her slowness.

bewail
destitute
detract
emancipate
extol
flamboyant
impetus
insuperable
intermittent
maxim
obligatory
plumb
vagabond
visage
wheedle

6. **insuperable**
   (a) There is no finer rose anywhere than the wild prairie rose.
   (b) No one has yet succeeded in rowing alone across the Pacific.
   (c) With five minutes to go, we were losing the basketball game by fifty points.

7. **visage**
   (a) My shoe size is 7 1/2 narrow.
   (b) I could tell at once that my answer had made her happy.
   (c) From this spot, you can see for miles in all directions.

8. **obligatory**
   (a) If you want to be on the committee, be at the next meeting.
   (b) Guests at White House state dinners must wear formal attire.
   (c) He finally had to admit that we were hopelessly lost.

9. **bewail**
   (a) Democracy doesn't work well with such a poor voter turnout.
   (b) From our cabin, we could hear the eerie howling of the wolves.
   (c) We'd all be better off if television had never been invented.

10. **maxim**
    (a) Neither a borrower nor a lender be.
    (b) Can you lend me five dollars until Friday?
    (c) Money burns a hole in his pocket.

1E Passage

Read the passage. Then answer the questions that follow it.

Faces in the Mountain

Visitors to South Dakota find that a trip to Mount Rushmore is almost **obligatory,** for there they can see one of America's most awe-inspiring monuments. Carved into a granite mountainside, the colossal heads of four United States presidents are visible for a distance of sixty miles. Side by side, the **visages** of George Washington, Thomas Jefferson, Abraham Lincoln, and Theodore Roosevelt range from fifty to seventy feet in height. They are the work of the remarkable American sculptor and dramatic personality Gutzon Borglum.

Born in Idaho in 1867, Borglum led an artist's **vagabond** life in America and Europe for twenty years before settling in New York City in 1901. There, he soon achieved an international reputation as a sculptor. The idea that "Small is beautiful" would not have applied to Borglum; his view was that "Bigger is better." In fact, it's said that he complained, "There is not a monument in this country as big as a snuff box."

The **impetus** for the Mount Rushmore project came in 1926, when the state historian of South Dakota, knowing Borglum's views, invited him to create a monumental work of art for the Black Hills mountain region. Borglum accepted the challenge immediately, but the project he proposed did not meet with universal approval. Many felt that the carvings would **detract** from the area's natural beauty. Cora Johnson, a South Dakota journalist, expressed such feelings when she wrote: "Man makes statues, but God made the mountains. Leave them alone." Borglum, however, was not one to heed this advice.

The question of which national figures to honor caused much debate. Sioux Chief Red Cloud, who had fought against white encroachment on Native American lands, was one of the names proposed. Another was Susan B. Anthony, who had **bewailed** nineteenth-century women's lack of the right to vote in political elections, and led the struggle to **emancipate** them from this deprivation. The final decision, however, was left to Borglum. Washington, Jefferson, and Lincoln were obvious choices, but Borglum had a personal reason for his fourth selection, a man of enormous energy who **extolled** physical fitness and vigorous activity. In his own life, Borglum strove to emulate his hero, so Theodore Roosevelt became the fourth figure honored at Mount Rushmore.

Money to pay for the project was a problem from the beginning, and work proceeded **intermittently,** especially after 1930, when the country was in the grip of the Great Depression. During those years, Borglum made frequent visits to the nation's capital seeking financial assistance. Loath to stoop to **wheedling,** the sculptor managed to convince a reluctant Congress to provide funding to go on with the project. Nor was lack of funds the only problem Borglum had to grapple with. Because of the hard granite rock, the difficulties of carving out the faces had at first seemed **insuperable,** but Borglum solved the problem by exploding small charges of dynamite to remove pieces of rock. Under his supervision, workers in harnesses suspended from the mountaintop drilled, chipped, and chiseled away at the rock. So skillful was Borglum that his eye for precise measurement enabled him to tell if a line was **plumb** to a quarter of an inch.

During his lifetime, Borglum had earned enormous sums from the sale of his works. However, he did not embrace Benjamin Franklin's **maxim** "A penny saved is a penny earned." Instead, he lived a **flamboyant** lifestyle. His daughter, Mary Ellis, recalls: "He loved flashy cars and hired chauffeurs to drive them." So careless was he about money that he died **destitute** on March 6, 1941. It was left to his son Lincoln, who had assisted him throughout, to complete the Mount Rushmore memorial eight months later.

bewail

destitute

detract

emancipate

extol

flamboyant

impetus

insuperable

intermittent

maxim

obligatory

plumb

vagabond

visage

wheedle

▶ **Answer each question in the form of a sentence. If a question does not contain a word from the lesson, use one in your answer. Use each word only once.**

1. Why might the original **detractors** of the Mount Rushmore project have a different view of it today?

_____

_____

2. Why would it be incorrect to refer to the Mount Rushmore sculptures as statues?

_____

_____

3. Why might a biographer of Borglum have difficulty describing what his subject was doing before 1901?

_____

_____

4. List two **maxims** that Borglum did not believe in.

_____

_____

5. Why was Susan B. Anthony considered a candidate for one of the places of honor on Mount Rushmore?

_____

_____

6. Why might Borglum's children have **bewailed** his **flamboyant** lifestyle?

_____

_____

7. What was the **impetus** for Borglum's trips to Washington, D.C., in the 1930s?

_____

_____

8. What were some of the almost **insuperable** problems Borglum encountered with this project?

_____

_____

9. What skill did Borglum possess that would be especially useful when working on a large monument such as Mount Rushmore?

_____

_____

10. How do you know that the state historian of South Dakota did not have to **wheedle** to get Borglum to take on the Mount Rushmore project?

_____

_____

11. Why might Borglum's son have felt it was **obligatory** to complete the monument?

_____

_____

FUN & FASCINATING FACTS

- A **flamboyant** person is someone who attracts attention by behaving in a showy way. The word *flamboyant* reflects this. It comes from the French verb *flamboyer*, which means "to blaze."

  The word *plumb* comes from the Latin root *plumbum*, meaning "lead." Some other words come from that root. One is *plumber*, a person who installs and repairs kitchen and bathroom pipes (which were once made of lead). The other is *plummet*, a verb meaning, "to fall straight down; to plunge." That meaning comes from the fact that a string with a lead weight attached to it is called a **plumb** line. It is lowered into the water and plunges, or plummets, to the bottom, giving a measure of depth.

bewail

destitute

detract

emancipate

extol

flamboyant

impetus

insuperable

intermittent

maxim

obligatory

plumb

vagabond

visage

wheedle

For more practice and games, go to www.WordlyWise3000.com.

Word List

Study the definitions of the words. Then do the exercises that follow.

alacrity
ə lak′ rə tē

n. 1. Promptness in responding.
The seller of the classic car accepted my first offer with such **alacrity** that I wished I had offered less.

2. Eagerness.
At the beginning of recess, the children ran to the playground with **alacrity.**

array
ə rā′

n. 1. A large group of people or things.
The ship's cabin contained an **array** of charts and maps.

2. An orderly arrangement or display.
The **array** of delectable sweets on the dessert tray tempted the diners.

v. 1. To place in order.
The marching band was **arrayed** at the entrance to the stadium for the Thanksgiving game.

2. To dress up.
The guests had **arrayed** themselves in elaborate attire for the Viennese ball.

deduce
dē dōōs′

v. To draw a conclusion from given facts.
Your carrying an umbrella leads me to **deduce** that you expect it to rain.

encumber
en kum′ bər

v. 1. To weigh down or burden.
I stumbled through the terminal door, **encumbered** by my two heavy suitcases.

2. To impede the action of.
Ice floes—large sheets of floating ice—**encumbered** the ships of early explorers in Antarctica.

encumbrance *n.*
Credit card debt was an **encumbrance** to the young couple as they struggled to save money for their first house.

fraught
frôt

adj. Full of or accompanied by (usually followed by *with*).
We abandoned our idea of traveling up the Amazon River when we learned that such a trip would be **fraught** with danger.

haphazard
hap haz′ ərd

adj. Marked by lack of plan, order, or direction.
He described in humorous detail his **haphazard** travels around Europe.

incontrovertible
in kän trə vərt′ ə bəl

adj. Impossible to dispute; unquestionable.
His statement that carbon dioxide levels in the atmosphere are increasing is **incontrovertible.**

inexplicable in eks pli´ kə bəl	*adj.* Hard to explain or impossible to understand. The disappearance of many ships and planes within the Atlantic Ocean's Bermuda Triangle is **inexplicable** to me.
ingenious in jēn´ yəs	*adj.* Marked by imagination, resourcefulness, or cleverness. Disposing of garbage by converting it into energy is an **ingenious** idea. **ingenuity** *n.* (in jə nōō´ ə tē) When she brought in her science project, the child's **ingenuity** was immediately apparent to her teachers.
laggard lag´ ərd	*n.* One who falls behind others because of moving slowly or loitering; a straggler. The **laggards** crossed the finish line long after the winner had broken the tape. *adj.* We have been **laggard** in getting the roof repaired.
sustenance sus´ tə nəns	*n.* Something that provides nourishment; food needed to live. Roots and berries provided **sustenance** for the sailors when the storm forced them to abandon ship and take refuge on the island.
torrid tôr´ id	*adj.* 1. Intensely hot and dry. It was impossible to walk barefoot on the **torrid** desert sand. 2. Burning with passion. The old letter was filled with **torrid** declarations of undying love.
traverse trə vʉrs´	*v.* To pass over, across, or through. Route 66, which **traverses** the United States from Chicago to Los Angeles, is sometimes called "The Mother Road" because in 1932 it opened the West to the automobile.
ubiquitous yōō bik´ wə təs	*adj.* Appearing to be present in large numbers or in many different places. Tourists with cameras are **ubiquitous** in Europe every summer.
zenith zē´ nith	*n.* 1. The highest point; the peak. Winning the Nobel prize for literature is, for some writers, the **zenith** of their career. 2. The point in the sky directly above the observer. Through the telescope, we spotted a comet that appeared to be midway between the horizon and the **zenith.**

Read the sentences. If a sentence correctly uses the word in bold, write C on the line. If a sentence is incorrect, rewrite it so that the vocabulary word in bold is used correctly.

1. To **encumber** someone is to load down that person, making it difficult for him to move.

   _____

   _____

2. An **ingenious** solution is one that requires mental agility.

   _____

   _____

3. The **zenith** of something is its lowest point.

   _____

   _____

4. To do something with **alacrity** is to do it in a dejected manner.

   _____

   _____

5. To **deduce** something is to cause it to happen.

   _____

   _____

6. To do something in a **haphazard** way is to do it in an organized way.

   _____

   _____

7. A journey **fraught** with risk is one that is not safe.

   _____

   _____

8. To **traverse** something is to do it over again.

   _____

   _____

9. **Sustenance** is something that supports life.

   _____

   _____

10. If something is **ubiquitous,** it is wicked or evil.

   _____

   _____

11. A **laggard** is a person who commits petty crimes.

   _____

   _____

12. If something is **inexplicable,** it is very puzzling.

_____

_____

13. An **array** of items is a list of them.

_____

_____

14. If something is **incontrovertible,** it cannot be defeated.

_____

_____

15. A **torrid** place is one that is very hot and dry.

_____

_____

2B ▶ Using Words

If the word (or a form of the word) in bold fits in a sentence in the group following it, write the word in the blank space. If the word does not fit, leave the space empty. There may be more than one correct answer.

1. **encumber**

   (a) Boulders strewn across the path _____ our progress through the woods.

   (b) We were advised not to _____ ourselves with too much equipment on our camping trip.

   (c) _____ with only a few possessions, we set off on our journey.

2. **alacrity**

   (a) With _____ Timmy headed across the room to take the last piece of cake.

   (b) At the Indianapolis "500," the racing car's _____ was clocked at over 150 mph.

   (c) Reading Stephen King's horror story *Pet Sematary* filled me with _____ .

3. **torrid**

   (a) The more _____ scenes were cut from the film to upgrade its rating.

   (b) Heat the water until it is _____ and then put the pasta in the pot.

   (c) The _____ noonday sun beat down unmercifully on the desert caravan.

alacrity
array
deduce
encumber
fraught
haphazard
incontrovertible
inexplicable
ingenious
laggard
sustenance
torrid
traverse
ubiquitous
zenith

4. **deduce**

    (a) The salesperson offered to _____ four-hundred dollars from the sticker price of the car.

    (b) I _____ from his disguise that he didn't want to be recognized.

    (c) If A equals B, and B equals C, then I _____ that A equals C.

5. **incontrovertible**

    (a) Sal was _____ when his parents told him they were getting a divorce.

    (b) Immigration and welfare are _____ subjects.

    (c) The evidence now seems _____ that smoking cigarettes causes lung cancer.

6. **fraught**

    (a) The journeys of nineteenth-century pioneers along the Oregon Trail were _____ with hardship.

    (b) Still feeling _____ from the flu, Mrs. Koza had to go and lie down.

    (c) According to my English teacher, the best poetry is _____ with emotional intensity.

7. **array**

    (a) The wedding party was _____ in formal attire.

    (b) The young women, _____ in long summery dresses, strolled through the gardens of the pre-Civil War plantation.

    (c) The jeweler laid out an _____ of rings for our inspection.

8. **laggard**

    (a) When the _____ showed up at the writing lab, they found that all the computers were in use.

    (b) My watch is _____ so I have to reset it every morning.

    (c) Although the tortoise was _____ , it still finished the race ahead of the hare.

Choose from the two words provided and use each word only once when filling in the spaces. One space should be left blank.

torrid / hot

1. The _____ waters off Greenland's coast were once rich in cod.

2. Temperatures on Venus reach a _____ 460 degrees Celsius.

3. As it gets _____ , iron begins to glow a dull red.

ingenious / clever

4. The _____ dog could sit, stay, and roll over on command.

5. The escape plan was so _____ that there was a good chance it would work.

6. When things start to get _____, it's time to go home.

extol / praise

7. They made a great effort to _____ the problem before it got bigger.

8. If you _____ people for good behavior, their manners may improve.

9. Most leaders _____ hard work as the best way to get ahead.

zenith / peak

10. Astronomers calculate the sky's _____ as ninety degrees above the horizon.

11. Demand for electricity reaches its _____ during very hot weather.

12. The bottom rung was broken, at the ladder's _____.

visage / face

13. Looking at the teacher's stern _____ reminded us to behave.

14. It's claimed that anti-aging cream applied to the _____ helps fight wrinkles.

15. The thin _____ of the mountain made it difficult to breathe.

alacrity
array
deduce
encumber
fraught
haphazard
incontrovertible
inexplicable
ingenious
laggard
sustenance
torrid
traverse
ubiquitous
zenith

Circle the letter of each sentence that suggests the numbered bold vocabulary word. In each group, you may circle more than one letter or none at all.

1. **encumbrance**

   (a) Wilma couldn't get a bank loan because she was already heavily in debt.

   (b) The backpack made it difficult for Brent to move quickly.

   (c) The painting was a gift for the Chins' wedding anniversary.

2. **ingenuity**

   (a) Mr. Asimov takes a great interest in his children's activities.

   (b) Learning to walk a tightrope takes a lot of practice.

   (c) Creating a seating plan that pleases everyone at the dinner party will not be easy.

3. **traverse**

   (a) I shifted into the wrong gear, and the car started to go backwards.

   (b) The George Washington Bridge connects New York and New Jersey.

   (c) The 1,200-mile journey across the polar ice cap took five weeks.

4. **haphazard**

   (a) The tent collapsed because Willy ignored the directions when putting it up.

   (b) The attendants made no attempt to line up the cars when parking them in the lot.

   (c) I tossed the coin into the air and it came down "heads."

5. **array**

   (a) I showed Charlie how to set up the chess pieces for the start of the game.

   (b) The performers all wore black and metallic silver outfits for the show.

   (c) The sea glowed with rosy light as the sun set.

6. **zenith**

   (a) After her one great success on Broadway, she disappeared from the limelight.

   (b) The road ran straight ahead for as far as the eye could see.

   (c) The flagpole cast no shadow even though the sun was shining.

7. **ubiquitous**

   (a) The sudden reappearance of the portrait stolen from the museum baffled us all.

   (b) You can hardly move in Florence, Italy, during the summer without bumping into tourists.

   (c) These rocks are over 350 million years old.

8. **sustenance**

   (a) Jamie's luck is bound to run out sooner or later.

   (b) While Elsie had the flu, she consumed only chicken soup, dry toast, water, and tea.

   (c) The beams in the ceiling help support the building.

9. **deduce**

   (a) Jonathan tried to subtract his portion from the total bill.
   (b) Fifteen minus eight equals seven.
   (c) Nothing you can say will persuade me to go on that roller coaster.

10. **inexplicable**

   (a) Scientists still wonder about the origin and purpose of a huge and ancient monument in Stonehenge, England.
   (b) My kitten became entangled in many feet of yarn and couldn't get free.
   (c) I've given up trying to figure out why Alex does the things he does.

2E Passage

Read the passage. Then answer the questions that follow it.

Survivors in the Sand

Ants, in existence for over a hundred million years, are some of the most **ubiquitous** of creatures. Ten thousand different species inhabit every part of the earth except the polar regions. None demonstrates the ability to adapt to hostile environments better than the tiny black desert ant of North Africa.

This small but apparently **ingenious** creature lives in underground burrows. It emerges only when it goes searching for other insects, which are its main form of **sustenance.** To do this, it may have to **traverse** an area extending for several hundred yards. Since it has no way of knowing where a dead insect might be found, the ant follows a **haphazard** path with frequent changes of direction. It is a task **fraught** with danger; no creature can survive for long in the **torrid** North African desert, where temperatures can climb to 160°F when the sun reaches its **zenith.** In such heat, the ant's life depends upon the **alacrity** with which it can accomplish its goal. And the black desert ant is no **laggard;** it can run over three hundred feet in less than two minutes—quite an achievement considering that its legs are a fraction of an inch long!

Having located a dead insect, the ant must return quickly to its burrow. This is no easy task for the ant, **encumbered** with a burden which may weigh more than it does. There is no time for the ant to start wondering in which direction it should head. Nor does it! What is remarkable about the black desert ant, and the reason it has aroused the interest of scientists, is its ability to return to its burrow directly, following the shortest possible route.

The desert's surface is quite featureless. So how does the ant know in which direction to go after it captures its prey? By studying the ant's brain and observing its behavior, entomologists—scientists who study insects—were able to **deduce** the answer to this question. They concluded that the ant's brain must store information about every change of direction, as well as the distances traveled.

alacrity
array
deduce
encumber
fraught
haphazard
incontrovertible
inexplicable
ingenious
laggard
sustenance
torrid
traverse
ubiquitous
zenith

Scientists found that the eyes of the black desert ant provide its brain with crucial information. Unlike human eyes, which have only a single lens, the eyes of the black desert ant contain an **array** of eighty lenses. These multiple lenses change the nature of the light passing through them, causing the light to become polarized. Polarized light vibrates in a single plane instead of scattering and vibrating in many planes at once, as is the case with light passing through a human eye. The polarized light is different for each area of the sky, so that every change in the ant's path alters the pattern of polarized light registered by the ant's brain. Should the ant turn, say, thirty degrees to the left, the changed pattern is recorded and stored in the ant's memory. This pattern then shows the ant its location relative to its burrow, thus enabling the ant to return there directly.

Scientists next tackled the seemingly **inexplicable** mystery of how the ant measures distance. A surprisingly simple experiment yielded the answer. They set up a narrow track along which the ant had to travel from its burrow. After going thirty feet in a single direction, the ant found a dead insect obligingly placed there by the scientists. The ant now wished to retrace its steps and return to its burrow; but instead, the scientists forced it to go back along a parallel track much longer than the first. After going thirty feet, the ant stopped and began searching for its burrow. To the scientists, this provided **incontrovertible** proof that the ant measures the distance it has traveled by "counting" its footsteps.

Not all ants have to cope with the hostile environment of the North African desert, but each species of ant is amazing in its own way and has developed its own strategy for survival. Considering what they have learned about insects such as ants, it's no wonder that many zoologists find entomology fascinating.

▶ **Answer each question in the form of a sentence. If a question does not contain a word from the lesson, use one in your answer. Use each word only once.**

1. What does the black desert ant's diet consist of?

_____

_____

2. In what significant way does the desert ant's eye differ from a human eye?

_____

_____

3. What exceptions are there to the statement that ants are **ubiquitous?**

_____

_____

4. Why is it unlikely that the black desert ant will be a **laggard** when it is out of the burrow during the middle of the day?

_____

_____

5. How would the desert ant's life be even more **fraught** with danger if it lost the use of its eyes?

_____

_____

6. In what way does the desert ant's return to the burrow with food differ from its journey outward in search of food?

_____

_____

7. Why did the ant's ability to find its way around in the desert seem **inexplicable** to scientists at first?

_____

_____

8. What did scientists **deduce** from the fact that the eyes of the desert ant have multiple lenses?

_____

_____

9. What is one detail from the passage that gives **incontrovertible** proof that desert ants have a brain?

_____

_____

10. According to the passage, what is the danger that black desert ants are likely to encounter when they leave their burrow?

_____

_____

11. What detail in the passage supports the statement that desert ants can move with **alacrity?**

_____

_____

12. Why is an ant's food such an **encumbrance?**

_____

_____

13. Give one example of **ingenuity** on the part of scientists in their study of ants.

_____

_____

alacrity
array
deduce
encumber
fraught
haphazard
incontrovertible
inexplicable
ingenious
laggard
sustenance
torrid
traverse
ubiquitous
zenith

- *Deduction,* meaning "the conclusion drawn by reasoning from a set of given facts," is the noun form of the verb **deduce.** (The discovery of the missing pearls confirms my *deduction* that they were mislaid and not stolen.) Note that *deduction* is also the noun form of the verb *deduct,* "to take an amount away from." (The fifty-dollar *deduction* from your wages is for taxes.)

- The earth is divided into five zones, or areas, according to climate and latitude. These zones are: two north and south frigid zones; two north and south temperate zones; and a fifth zone that straddles the equator called, not surprisingly, the **torrid** zone.

- The word **zenith** comes from the Arabic *samt,* which means "path" or "way." It passed into Medieval Latin, the universal language of learning in the Middle Ages, then into English as *senyth* before acquiring its modern spelling. (As it travels a path across the sky, the sun reaches its *zenith* at a point directly above the observer.) The antonym of *zenith* is *nadir,* meaning "the point in the sky directly opposite the zenith" or "the lowest point." (Allied hopes for victory over Nazi Germany were at their *nadir* in 1940.)

For more practice and games, go to **www.WordlyWise3000.com**.

Word List	Study the definitions of the words. Then do the exercises that follow.

allude
a lōōd´

v. To refer to in an indirect way (used with *to*).
"I made a mistake that night," he said, **alluding** to the way he lost his temper.

allusion *n.*
The poem "An Ancient Gesture," by Edna St. Vincent Millay, is an **allusion** to Penelope in Homer's *The Odyssey*.

consecrate
kän´ sə krāt

v. 1. To set apart as holy.
Hagia Sophia, in Constantinople (today Istanbul), was **consecrated** as a church in 537 and is now a museum.

2. To dedicate to a cause; to devote.
Mother Teresa **consecrated** her life to helping Calcutta's poor.

disseminate
di səm´ i nāt

v. To scatter or spread widely.
The wind **disseminated** the spores from the milkweed pods.

dissemination *n.*
Dissemination of information about the transmission of HIV infection is essential for preventing AIDS.

dote
dōt

v. To show excessive fondness for (used with *on* or *upon*).
She **dotes** on her grandson and indulges his every whim.

exhort
eg zôrt´

v. To urge strongly; to warn or appeal.
His wife **exhorted** him to ignore the urgings of the salesman at the boatyard.

exhortation *n.*
The Bhagavad-Gita, a text sacred to Hindus, contains **exhortations** for humans to do their duty.

feckless
fek´ ləs

adj. Careless or irresponsible.
Pip's **feckless** ways in London left him devoid of cash.

implicate
im´ pli kāt´

v. To show to be involved with something, especially something dishonest or illegal.
The defense attorney insisted that her client could not be **implicated** in the theft.

lament
lə ment´

v. To feel or express grief.
Uncountable mourners lined the streets to **lament** the 1997 death of Diana, Princess of Wales.

lamentation (or **lament**) *n.* An expression of sorrow or grief in the form of a poem, song, etc.
"Natalia," sung by Joan Baez, is a **lamentation** for an especially brave political prisoner in the former Czechoslovakia.

monetary män´ ə ter´ ē	*adj.* Of or relating to money or currency. The basic **monetary** unit of Mexico is the peso.
pensive pen´ siv	*adj.* Deep in thought; dreamily thoughtful. Lying on my back, I grew **pensive** as I watched the drifting summer clouds.
pomp pämp	*n.* A showy or dignified display. The commencement exercises at major universities are usually marked by **pomp** and ceremony.
stilted stil´ təd	*adj.* Artificially stiff or formal in manner. His **stilted** conversation reflected his unease at the gathering of artists in the gallery.
subjugate sub´ jə gāt	*v.* To bring under control; to conquer. In the late eighteenth century, Russia **subjugated** the country of Georgia, in western Asia, and made it part of the Russian empire. **subjugation** *n.* The organization Amnesty International received the Nobel Peace Prize for "its efforts on behalf of defending human dignity against violence and **subjugation**."
trauma trô´ mə	*n.* 1. A severe bodily injury. The accident victims who suffered **trauma** were airlifted to major hospitals for emergency services. 2. Emotional shock. Nguyen Hui survived the **trauma** of fleeing Vietnam by boat in 1979 and eventually settled in the United States. **traumatic** *adj.* Simply watching on television the devastation resulting from the bombing in Oklahoma City had a **traumatic** effect on me.
wanton wänt´ n	*adj.* 1. Ignoring what is right. In refusing to remove asbestos from the ceilings, the company showed a **wanton** disregard for its employees' health and safety. 2. Excessive or unrestrained. During the holidays, I try to avoid **wanton** eating of sweets. 3. Playful or frolicsome. It was a pleasure to hear the **wanton** shouts of the children in the backyard.

Read the sentences. If a sentence correctly uses the word in bold, write *C* on the line. If a sentence is incorrect, rewrite it so that the vocabulary word in bold is used correctly.

1. A **pensive** mood is one that engrosses a person in thought.

   _____

   _____

2. To **implicate** is to beg a person to do something.

   _____

   _____

3. **Pomp** is a brilliant spectacle.

   _____

   _____

4. **Subjugation** is the act of overpowering a person or group.

   _____

   _____

5. To **consecrate** a place is to make it sacred.

   _____

   _____

6. A **stilted** manner is one that seems forced and unnatural.

   _____

   _____

7. An **allusion** is a mistaken belief.

   _____

   _____

8. **Wanton** insults are those that are wildly improper and uncontrolled.

   _____

   _____

9. A **monetary** concern is one that changes frequently.

   _____

   _____

10. To **exhort** someone is to obtain something by threatening that person.

    _____

    _____

11. A **traumatic** incident is one that has unimaginable consequences.

    _____

    _____

allude
consecrate
disseminate
dote
exhort
feckless
implicate
lament
monetary
pensive
pomp
stilted
subjugate
trauma
wanton

12. **Dissemination** is the act of distinguishing between right and wrong.

_____

_____

13. To **dote** on someone is to show a strong affection for that person.

_____

_____

14. A **feckless** person is one who doesn't take ordinary precautions.

_____

_____

15. A **lament** is an expression of sorrow.

_____

_____

3B ▶ Using Words

If the word (or a form of the word) in bold fits in a sentence in the group following it, write the word in the blank space. If the word does not fit, leave the space empty. There may be more than one correct answer.

1. **exhort**

   (a) By the third day of our journey, our supplies were _____ .

   (b) The leader of the protest march _____ his followers to be patient, but they did not heed him.

   (c) Mrs. Dalloway _____ her nephew to pass her the sugar.

2. **subjugate**

   (a) Everyone expects Levertov to _____ her opponent in tomorrow's tennis match.

   (b) I was determined not to let the difficulty of the task _____ me.

   (c) During the Civil War, the North's efforts to _____ the South were concluded at the village of Appomattox Court House in Virginia.

3. **consecrate**

   (a) In his address at the dedication of the Gettysburg National Cemetery, Abraham Lincoln said that the men who fought and died there had already _____ the land.

   (b) The physician Tom Dooley (1927–61) _____ his life to philanthropic work in Indochina.

   (c) Joe was sleepy and found it hard to _____ on the math problem.

4. **wanton**

   (a) He laughingly threatened revenge for their _____ practical jokes.

   (b) To keep those big dogs in that small apartment was _____ cruelty.

   (c) Maria believed in doing good by performing _____ acts of kindness.

5. **pomp**

   (a) A royal wedding is an occasion for much _____

   (b) Thomas Jefferson was not impressed by the _____ of the French court.

   (c) These women's suits lack _____ and are appropriate for business wear.

6. **feckless**

   (a) The couple's _____ spending resulted in their decision to declare bankruptcy.

   (b) One could easily get lost in the _____ wastes of the desert.

   (c) The _____ father had failed to pay child support for over two years.

7. **implicate**

   (a) Robert could not have acted alone, but he refused to _____ his friends.

   (b) The campaign will _____ a lot of planning if it is to be a success.

   (c) She tried to _____ the sobbing child by hugging him.

8. **pensive**

   (a) A _____ look crossed her face whenever we spoke of Cuba, the land of her birth.

   (b) It was _____ of her to go to so much trouble on my behalf.

   (c) The music's more _____ movements were played with great feeling.

allude

consecrate

disseminate

dote

exhort

feckless

implicate

lament

monetary

pensive

pomp

stilted

subjugate

trauma

wanton

Complete the analogies by selecting the pair of words whose relationship most resembles the relationship of the pair in capital letters. Circle the letter in front of the pair you choose.

1. INJURY : TRAUMA ::
   (a) luck : skill
   (b) illness : medicine
   (c) visage : eyes
   (d) accident : calamity

2. ADORE : DOTE ::
   (a) attempt : succeed
   (b) lament : bewail
   (c) deduce : misunderstand
   (d) explain : implicate

3. WANTON : RESTRAINT ::
   (a) ignorant : awareness
   (b) pensive : thought
   (c) silent : guilt
   (d) dangerous : risk

4. DISSEMINATE : ACCUMULATE ::
   (a) dismay : alarm
   (b) dissent : disagree
   (c) distribute : collect
   (d) flatter : extol

5. RARE : UBIQUITOUS ::
   (a) feckless : reckless
   (b) intermittent : continuous
   (c) hidden: unseen
   (d) several : many

6. PROTEIN: SUSTENANCE ::
   (a) bricks : house
   (b) air : lungs
   (c) oil : heat
   (d) book : reader

7. DESTITUTE : MONEY ::
   (a) wise : wisdom
   (b) tired : sleep
   (c) funny : laughter
   (d) thirsty : hunger

8. PLUMB : LEVEL ::
   (a) deep : shallow
   (b) front : back
   (c) firm : wobbly
   (d) vertical : horizontal

9. BEWAIL : MISFORTUNE ::
   (a) ignore : knowledge
   (b) rejoice : victory
   (c) subjugate : enemy
   (d) extol : fear

10. FLAMBOYANT : DULL ::
    (a) feckless : responsible
    (b) snowy : white
    (c) pensive : thoughtful
    (d) formal : stilted

Circle the letter of each sentence that suggests the numbered bold vocabulary word. In each group, you may circle more than one letter or none at all.

1. **lament**
   (a) "I can't believe that I'll never see you again," he said sadly.
   (b) In the theatrical production of the Greek myth, singers wailed over the deaths of Medea's children.
   (c) "I'm sorry I can't give you directions," she said, "but I'm a stranger here myself."

2. **subjugate**
   (a) Sixteen minus eleven is five.
   (b) By 1224, Genghis Khan had extended his empire over most of Asia.
   (c) Lena always puts herself first.

3. **allusion**
   (a) Natasha's unfailing optimism prompted her negative cousin to call her a Pollyanna.
   (b) Her parents named her Simone after her grandmother.
   (c) His reputation for being stingy earned him the nickname of Scrooge.

4. **monetary**
   (a) A fifty-dollar reward was offered to anyone who could find the lost dog.
   (b) The actions of the Federal Reserve System affect interest rates in the United States.
   (c) The dollar rose in value against the German mark and the Japanese yen.

5. **trauma**
   (a) Many Vietnam veterans have emotional problems as a result of their experiences in the war.
   (b) The motorcyclist suffered severe head injuries in the accident.
   (c) Little Tómas started screaming when he dropped his ice cream cone.

6. **exhortation**
   (a) Her fans cheered wildly when tennis player Steffi Graf won Wimbledon.
   (b) Get a good night's rest before taking the SATs.
   (c) Mother lost count of the times she asked Nigel to clean up his room.

7. **stilted**
   (a) "I must request of you that you cease trespassing upon my property," said the landholder.
   (b) "Chill out," drawled Becky to her angry sister.
   (c) Are you familiar with the line "Hark! The meadowlark doth greet the morn"?

8. **disseminate**
   (a) The boys fled in all directions when they saw Mr. Garroway approaching.
   (b) Every home in Miami Dade County, Florida, received a "Hurricane Information" package.
   (c) Banned literature was circulated in communist Russia in a system called *samizdat*.

allude
consecrate
disseminate
dote
exhort
feckless
implicate
lament
monetary
pensive
pomp
stilted
subjugate
trauma
wanton

9. **consecrate**

   (a) The parlor of the guest house was used as a reading room.

   (b) Art's first job was stockboy in a warehouse.

   (c) Melissa kept a daily record of personal events in a closely guarded journal.

10. **dote**

    (a) Walter plays with his Krime Kruncher video game for hours at a time.

    (b) "Oh, I think Rachel's the best girl in the world!" said Aunt Penny.

    (c) Jacob could do no wrong in his grandparents' eyes.

3E Passage

Read the passage. Then answer the questions that follow it.

Chile's First Lady of Letters

By order of the government, the country went into three days of mourning. All schools and official buildings were closed. Flags were lowered to half-mast. Was the nation **lamenting** the passing of a president or a famous general? No. The person whose death was being marked with such **pomp** was a poet. The country was Chile; the year was 1957; and the poet was Gabriela Mistral, born Lucila Godoy Alcayaga sixty-eight years earlier.

Lucila grew up in Chile's Valley of Elqui, a place she **alludes** to frequently in her poems as an earthly paradise of vineyards, fig orchards, and green hills. Her father **doted** on his child, making a garden for Lucila and listening with delight as she talked to the flowers, birds, and insects. But his **feckless** ways and frequent absences caused quarrels between Lucila's parents. When the little girl was three, her father disappeared from her life forever. Friends remembered her as a solitary child whose **pensive** ways cut her off from companionship. She compensated for this by creating a rich interior world for herself. By the age of eleven, she was writing her first poems.

When she was a young woman, two unhappy love affairs brought **trauma** to Lucila's life. In one case, the young man committed suicide after being **implicated** in a crime; in the other, a woman from a wealthy Santiago family abruptly replaced Lucila in the affections of the man she had hoped to marry. Believing that marriage and motherhood were not in her future, she **consecrated** her life to teaching, a calling she held in the highest regard, and writing poetry. Taking the pen name Gabriela Mistral, she poured her grief into her poetry: "Though you creep to the corners of the earth to kiss her, you will see my tearstained face."

Hers was a fresh voice, sometimes direct, even harsh; other times it was tender and wistful, offering quite a contrast to the often **stilted** language of some of her contemporaries. In 1922, Mistral received international recognition with the publication of *Desolación* [*Desolation*]. This was a volume of poetry pervaded by a sense of suffering and lost love, and with scorn for indifference to pain and excessive emphasis on materialism. Mistral used her new-found celebrity to **disseminate** her views on education, which began appearing in newspapers and journals throughout the Americas. An invitation to visit Mexico to advise leaders there on educational reform, and an appointment as "consul for life" for the Chilean government began Mistral's life of travel. The salary she received from her official position enabled her to pursue her literary and educational activities free of **monetary** worries.

Whatever her activity, concern for children, nature, and the downtrodden filled her mind. Her second book, *Ternura* [*Tenderness*], contains many children's songs and verses that reflect her study of folk verse, nursery rhymes, and lullabies. Next came *Tala* [*The Felling of Trees*], a reference to the **wanton** destruction of Chile's forests by greedy timber barons. She assigned the proceeds from *Tala* to the relief of children orphaned by the Spanish Civil War after her **exhortations** to the countries of South America to take in refugees from Spain went unheeded. In 1945, Gabriela Mistral was awarded the Nobel Prize for Literature. She was the first Latina writer to be so honored. In her acceptance speech, she expressed her thanks on behalf of writers of "the southern hemisphere of the American continent, so little and so poorly known."

Now a world figure, Mistral traveled extensively in Europe and throughout the Americas. She taught, wrote, and spoke out in public on behalf of the world's children who were denied education and forced to work in appalling conditions for low wages. Unhappy about the **subjugation** of women in much of the world, she served on the United Nations committee on the Status of Women. At the same time, she expressed "highest admiration" for the achievements of women of the United States and lived there for a time. She was staying with friends on Long Island when she died on January 10, 1957.

In Santiago, the honor guard at Gabriela Mistral's funeral was composed of four hundred children—a procession appropriate for a woman whose heart adopted the children of the whole world and celebrated them in her poetry: "Rivers are circles of children/Running off to the sea as they play/Waves are circlets of little girls/ Embracing the world as they play."

▶ **Answer each question in the form of a sentence. If a question does not contain a word from the lesson, use one in your answer. Use each word only once.**

1. What contradiction do you see in the way Mistral's father treated her?

   _____

   _____

2. How did the **traumas** of Mistral's childhood and early adulthood influence the direction of her life?

   _____

   _____

allude
consecrate
disseminate
dote
exhort
feckless
implicate
lament
monetary
pensive
pomp
stilted
subjugate
trauma
wanton

3. Why did Mistral's poems seem revolutionary at the time she wrote them?

_____

_____

4. How do you know that the Valley of Elqui, where Mistral grew up, had a long-lasting effect on her?

_____

_____

5. Why would it be inaccurate to describe Mistral as a **wanton** child?

_____

_____

6. Whom did Mistral **implicate** in her collection of poems, *Tala*?

_____

_____

7. How do we know that Mistral's writing was not motivated solely by **monetary** considerations?

_____

_____

8. Why might Mistral have considered South American countries **feckless** in their treatment of refugees from the Spanish Civil War?

_____

_____

9. How did Mistral make known her views on mistreated children?

_____

_____

10. What problems did Mistral see afflicting women and children?

_____

_____

11. Why do you think so many **lamented** the death of Gabriela Mistral?

_____

_____

12. What part did children play in the **pomp** that attended Mistral's funeral?

_____

_____

Don't confuse *allude* with *elude* or *allusion* with *illusion*. *Elude* means "to avoid or escape from" (*elude* the hounds); an *illusion* is a mistaken idea (existing under the *illusion* that she would return) or a sight or image that deceives the eye. (Paintings with black and white shapes that appear to move are optical *illusions*.)

One might think that to be **feckless** is to lack "feck," an assumption that leads to the question, "What is *feck*?" *Feck* is an old Scottish word meaning "effect." From this information, we can see how "ineffective" as a meaning of *feckless* makes sense.

A person using **stilted** language can be thought of as trying to raise her speech to a higher level in a way that does not come naturally to her. Such behavior can be compared to a person who raises himself above others by walking on stilts. Stilted language results in stiff, awkward expression, while walking on stilts produces stiff, awkward movement.

allude

consecrate

disseminate

dote

exhort

feckless

implicate

lament

monetary

pensive

pomp

stilted

subjugate

trauma

wanton

Lesson 4

Word List	Study the definitions of the words. Then do the exercises that follow.
adage ad´ ij	*n.* An old saying that has come to be accepted as true; a proverb. Preparing to move again, I comforted myself with the **adage** "A rolling stone gathers no moss."
camaraderie käm´ ə räd´ ər ē	*n.* Good will and warm feelings among friends. A spirit of **camaraderie** filled the room where the group gathered for its high-school reunion.
contend kən tend´	*v.* 1. To struggle with. Mail carriers sometimes have to **contend** with bothersome dogs. 2. To maintain or assert. Opponents of nuclear power plants **contend** that the risk of a malfunction in one is too great. **contention** *n.* 1. A conflict or struggle. Miwa and Jessie are in **contention** for first place on the honor roll. 2. A point made in an argument. It is my **contention** that the ghost you claim to have seen was merely a shadow on the wall.
extraneous ek strä´ nē əs	*adj.* Not necessary; irrelevant. When you revise your written instructions, eliminate any **extraneous** details.
hubbub hu´ bub	*n.* Noisy confusion; uproar. Fans thronged onto the field in a **hubbub** of excitement when the Boston Red Sox won the pennant.
meander mē an´ dər	*v.* 1. To follow a winding course. The Mississippi River **meanders** from northern Minnesota to the Gulf of Mexico. 2. To wander aimlessly. Shoppers at the sidewalk sale **meandered** through the street looking for bargains.
odoriferous ō dər if´ ər əs	*adj.* Having or giving off a smell. **Odoriferous** fumes spewed from the truck's exhaust.
paraphernalia per ə fər nāl´ yə	*n.* 1. Personal belongings. We accumulated so much **paraphernalia** that the closets couldn't hold it all. 2. Equipment associated with a particular activity. We keep our riding **paraphernalia** in the barn.

punctilious puŋk til´ ē əs	*adj.* Careful of and attentive to details, especially ones relating to good manners and behavior. A **punctilious** host tries to leave nothing to chance when preparing for guests.
recuperate rē kōō´ pər āt´	*v.* To regain health or strength. Her surgeon expects Amanda to **recuperate** quickly.
regale rē gāl´	*v.* To entertain or delight. Charlie **regaled** the guests with his funny stories.
sedentary sed´ n ter´ ē	*adj.* Doing or requiring a lot of sitting. Operating a computer is **sedentary** work.
Spartan spärt´ n	*adj.* Marked by simplicity and lack of luxury. The Marine sergeant described the **Spartan** way of life at the recruits' training camp.
temporal tem´ pər əl	*adj.* Relating to the everyday world as opposed to that which is spiritual or eternal. Medieval kings were the **temporal** rulers of their states, but in religious matters they accepted the Pope's authority.
wry rī	*adj.* 1. Turned or bent to one side in distaste or humor. He gave a **wry** smile as he admitted believing such a far-fetched tale. 2. Amusing in a quiet but sharp way. The poem's **wry** wit made me smile inwardly.

4A ▷ Understanding Meanings

Read the sentences. If a sentence correctly uses the word in bold, write *C* on the line. If a sentence is incorrect, rewrite it so that the vocabulary word in bold is used correctly.

1. To **meander** is to move directly from one place to another.

_____

_____

2. A **sedentary** occupation is one that requires much traveling.

_____

_____

3. An **extraneous** matter is one that is not related to the topic at hand.

_____

_____

4. An **adage** is a new section attached to an old house.

_____

_____

5. An **odoriferous** substance is one that produces a scent.

_____

_____

6. To **contend** something is to claim that it is so.

_____

_____

7. A **wry** facial expression is one with a slight twist to it.

_____

_____

8. A **punctilious** person is one who is frequently late.

_____

_____

9. To **regale** a crowd is to make the people in it laugh.

_____

_____

10. A **hubbub** is a kind of bath oil.

_____

_____

11. **Camaraderie** is a type of march appropriate for a parade.

_____

_____

12. To **recuperate** is to return to one's place of departure.

_____

_____

13. **Paraphernalia** consists of items needed for a special undertaking.

_____

_____

14. **Temporal** affairs are those concerned with material rather than spiritual matters.

_____

_____

15. A **Spartan** diet is one that excludes meat and meat products.

_____

_____

If the word (or a form of the word) in bold fits in a sentence in the group following it, write the word in the blank space. If the word does not fit, leave the space empty. There may be more than one correct answer.

1. **odoriferous**

   (a) An _____ sight met my eyes when I opened the door.

   (b) The _____ perfume of honeysuckle on the vine brings back childhood memories.

   (c) _____ bags of garbage lay on the sidewalk waiting to be collected.

2. **contend**

   (a) Do you still _____ that the first Olympic Games were held in 76 B.C.E.?

   (b) Sixteen teams _____ for the title of national champion.

   (c) The sailboats had to _____ with strong winds on the first leg of the race.

3. **wry**

   (a) I had pastrami on _____ bread for lunch.

   (b) Alyssa took a sip from the glass of cider and made a _____ face as she set it down.

   (c) Maxwell broke the uncomfortable silence by interjecting a comment spiced with his _____ sense of humor.

4. **temporal**

   (a) I made a _____ repair in the bathroom and hoped it would last until the plumber came.

   (b) The preacher stressed the importance of spiritual matters rather than _____ ones.

   (c) The ethics book deals with _____ matters, avoiding all religious questions.

5. **regale**

   (a) The actress who played Catherine the Great made a truly _____ entrance.

   (b) Uncle Boris loved to _____ his guests with mystifying card tricks.

   (c) It would _____ me greatly if you would accept this invitation.

6. **camaraderie**

   (a) What I enjoyed most about summer camp was the _____ between counselors and campers.

   (b) A feeling of _____ soon developed among the members of the cast.

   (c) Julius seems to have lost his _____ and has gone off alone.

adage
camaraderie
contend
extraneous
hubbub
meander
odoriferous
paraphernalia
punctilious
recuperate
regale
sedentary
Spartan
temporal
wry

7. **hubbub**

   (a) The _____ created by my younger sister and her friends in the next room made it impossible for me to concentrate on my math assignment.

   (b) The two girls patched up their _____ and agreed to be friends again.

   (c) The _____ died down when the judge entered the courtroom.

8. **recuperate**

   (a) We could hear the coffee _____ , so we knew it was ready.

   (b) I went to my grandmother's to _____ after my operation.

   (c) I told her to _____ all her good fortune and stop feeling sorry for herself.

4c ▶ Word Study

Change each of the verbs into a noun by changing, adding, or dropping the suffix. Write the word in the space provided.

Verb	Noun
1. emancipate	_____
2. disseminate	_____
3. exhort	_____
4. lament	_____
5. subjugate	_____
6. contend	_____

Change each of the adjectives into a noun by changing, adding, or dropping the suffix. Write the word in the space provided.

Adjective	Noun
7. destitute	_____
8. flamboyant	_____
9. ingenious	_____
10. traumatic	_____

Circle the letter of each sentence that suggests the numbered bold vocabulary word. In each group, you may circle more than one letter or none at all.

1. **contention**
   (a) I still say that our soccer team has a chance of winning the championship.
   (b) Students and faculty disagree over the proposed dress code.
   (c) Maisie liked nothing better than to curl up with a good book.

2. **adage**
   (a) The early bird catches the worm.
   (b) Haste makes waste.
   (c) Wait here until I get back.

3. **punctilious**
   (a) This is the third flat tire I've had in less than a week.
   (b) As soon as I got up off the sofa, Marjorie straightened out the cushions.
   (c) I told Jed to forget about it, but he insisted on paying me back the dollar.

4. **Spartan**
   (a) The room contained only a bed, a chest of drawers, and a lamp.
   (b) We lived mostly on bread and potatoes with an occasional piece of fruit.
   (c) There was nothing to read but some old magazines and romance novels.

5. **sedentary**
   (a) Every hour or so, Robertson left his desk to do some stretching exercises.
   (b) I took some medicine for my headache and continued my walk.
   (c) Layers of sand on the ocean floor formed these sandstone cliffs.

6. **paraphernalia**
   (a) The fans went crazy when the referee made the call.
   (b) The Genoveses' fishhooks, nylon line, sinkers, and lures were kept in the tackle box.
   (c) A pen and some paper are all that a poet needs.

7. **meander**
   (a) The flock of geese took off from the pond and headed south.
   (b) The tourists made their way around Chicago on foot, taking in the many sights.
   (c) We crossed the river at a number of points, going from one side to the other.

8. **camaraderie**
   (a) It took over an hour to put the scattered papers back in order.
   (b) From his earliest years, Joshua was very talkative.
   (c) Although I had just met the captain, there was something about him that made me trust him.

adage

camaraderie

contend

extraneous

hubbub

meander

odoriferous

paraphernalia

punctilious

recuperate

regale

sedentary

Spartan

temporal

wry

9. **extraneous**

  (a) Last week, I made fifty dollars more than my regular pay by working overtime.

  (b) What Caroline told him is beside the point and need not concern us.

  (c) You don't need to take your overcoat on a Caribbean vacation.

10. **wry**

  (a) Do you think that this milk has a funny taste?

  (b) The wire had became so twisted that it was difficult to move the phone across the room.

  (c) When I asked a worried-looking Karl if he needed help, he replied, "No. I'm doing fine."

4E Passage

Read the passage. Then answer the questions that follow it.

The Longest Journey

An old **adage** states that the longest journey begins with a single step. If the journey is along the length of the 2,144-mile Appalachian National Scenic Trail, that step will be followed by approximately five million more! The trail stretches primarily along the crest of the Appalachian Mountains from Springer Mountain, Georgia, to Mount Katahdin, Maine. Known as "the longest footpath in the world," it **meanders** through fourteen states along the Atlantic seaboard. Virtually all the land over which the trail passes is owned by the National Park Service. The trail itself, however, is privately managed by thirty-one Appalachian Trail Clubs. These clubs, whose members are all volunteers, are **punctilious** about maintaining the trail and its markers; they also provide the **Spartan** shelters located a day's hike apart along its length.

Several million people walk a part of the Appalachian Trail each year. A hundred or so travel its entire length. It takes them up to half a year to do so. These "thru-hikers" include people from all walks of life. They range in age from teenagers to people in their seventies and older. A retired admiral, a couple on a six-month honeymoon walk, and a veteran hiker who has traveled the trail a half-dozen times may find themselves bedding down in the same shelter at the end of the day to **recuperate** from six or eight hours of strenuous walking. As the sun goes down, hikers enjoy the **camaraderie** that develops among those enjoying a common experience. They can rub their sore feet, share the food they carry in their backpacks, and **regale** each other with stories of the day's adventures.

Perhaps the most remarkable "thru-hiker" is Bill Irwin. Irwin's eight-month adventure began when he set off from Springer Mountain in the early spring of 1990. It ended when he reached Mount Katahdin on November 22. Because his trip took longer than most, he had to **contend** with ghastly weather conditions toward the end. Such conditions included one-hundred-miles-per-hour wind gusts and a blizzard that dumped two feet of snow on the trail. The reason his hike was so long and slow is that Irwin is a blind person. He was accompanied only by Orient, his seeing eye dog. In a **wry** allusion, Irwin referred to himself and his companion as "the Orient Express."

The trail's rustic charm is one of its main attractions. Although Irwin was unable to enjoy the splendid mountain views it affords, his other senses are so highly developed that through listening, feeling, and smelling, he believes he missed very little. He couldn't see the white two-by-six-inch markers painted on trees and rocks that identify the trail, but he was never in danger of getting lost. To Orient, whose sense of smell is unusually well developed, it was easy to follow the **odoriferous** trail—filled with the smells of foliage, earth, and other hikers and their belongings.

What is it that draws people to the Appalachian Trail? Some seek the challenge of exchanging a **sedentary** lifestyle for one that tests their strength and will to the limit. For such people, success can be exhilarating. Carrying a fifty-pound backpack crammed with hiking **paraphernalia** while trudging with wet blistered feet up a steep hill in a heavy downpour might not seem like fun. Those who have done it, however, say that to dwell on such times is to miss the point. Satisfaction comes from coping with whatever nature brings.

Other hikers set out to escape the **hubbub** of the city for a few days, weeks, or months of solitude in the wilderness. As they ignore minor physical discomforts, they say that they can escape **temporal** concerns and reflect upon what is essential and what is **extraneous** in their lives.

Most set out from Springer Mountain and head north, but regardless of the direction hikers travel, many say that the inner journey they experience is the most important one.

▶ **Answer each question in the form of a sentence. If a question does not contain a word from the lesson, use one in your answer. Use each word only once.**

1. Why do hikers owe a debt of gratitude to Appalachian Trail Club members?

   _____

   _____

2. Why is the actual trail longer than the distance from Springer Mountain to Mount Katahdin?

   _____

   _____

3. What are some of the things that hikers might have to **contend** with?

   _____

   _____

adage

camaraderie

contend

extraneous

hubbub

meander

odoriferous

paraphernalia

punctilious

recuperate

regale

sedentary

Spartan

temporal

wry

4. What does the term "**Spartan** shelters" suggest?

_____

_____

5. Why was Bill Irwin not in danger of getting lost on the trail?

_____

_____

6. What **adage** about dogs would describe Bill Irwin's relationship with Orient?

_____

_____

7. Why is "the Orient Express" described as a **wry** expression?

_____

_____

8. Why is it likely that "thru-hikers" would develop a special **camaraderie?**

_____

_____

9. What aspect of life in the city is absent from life on the Appalachian Trail?

_____

_____

10. What **paraphernalia** would a hiker be likely to take on a trip?

_____

_____

11. How are the hikers likely to spend their evenings in the shelters?

_____

_____

12. According to the passage, what are two reasons that people might hike the Appalachian Trail?

_____

_____

- Since an *adage* is an old saying that has come to be accepted as true, there can be no such thing as a young or recent *adage*. Anyone using the expression "According to the old **adage…**" is being careless in the use of language.

- The Gaelic phrase *ub ub ubub* was an expression of contempt that the English converted for their own use to **hubbub,** "a noisy uproar."

  The early European settlers in New England gave the name *hubbub* to a game, similar to a dice game, played with bones on a tray and popular among Native Americans of the region. The name suggests that it must have been accompanied by much shouting and excitement.

- The Maender River in Phrygia, now part of modern Turkey, made its way with many twists and turns on its way to the sea. Its name became associated with anything that takes a winding course and gave us the modern English verb **meander.**

- The ancient city-state Sparta was the capital of Laconia, in southern Greece. Under strict military leadership, Sparta's people were trained rigorously to endure great hardship and to lead frugal lives. (Sparta eventually defeated its rival Athens in 404 B.C.E.) The people of Laconia were noted for being sparing of speech, so they contributed not only the adjective **Spartan** to the English language, but also the word *laconic*, meaning "using few words."

adage

camaraderie

contend

extraneous

hubbub

meander

odoriferous

paraphernalia

punctilious

recuperate

regale

sedentary

Spartan

temporal

wry

Crossword Puzzle Solve the crossword puzzle by studying the clues and filling in the answer boxes. Clues followed by a number are definitions of words in Lessons 1 through 4. The number gives the word list in which the answer to the clue appears.

Clues Across

1. Without resources or possessions (1)
7. To express deep regret or sorrow over (1)
10. To pass over, across, or through (2)
12. Combination of red and yellow
13. An expression of sorrow (3)
14. Slow to act or respond (2)
16. To show excessive fondness for (3)
18. To take away the value of (1)
20. A general truth or rule; a short saying (1)
21. Opposite of spend
23. To measure the depth of water (1)
24. Amusing in a quiet but sharp way (4)
25. _____ and Juliet
26. Former unit of money in France
27. Greatest in age
28. A driving force (1)

Clues Down

2. To praise highly (1)
3. Causing severe bodily injury or emotional shock (3)
4. Careless or irresponsible (3)
5. Hawaiian greeting
6. To follow a winding course (4)
8. An old saying that is accepted as true (4)
9. Doing or requiring a lot of sitting (4)
11. To urge strongly, to warn or appeal (3)
15. Material or everyday; not spiritual (4)
17. Full of or accompanied by (2)
18. Drew a conclusion from given facts (2)
19. Intensely hot and dry (2)
22. An orderly arrangement or display (2)
23. A showy or dignified display (3)
24. North, east, south, _____

Lesson 5

Word List	Study the definitions of the words. Then do the exercises that follow.

callow
kal´ ō

adj. Young and inexperienced; immature.
The student was too **callow** to know he was being fooled.

contemporary
kən tem´ pər er´ ē

n. A person living during the same period as another.
Martha Jane Canary, known as "Calamity Jane," and Annie Oakley were **contemporaries.**

adj. Existing or occurring at the same time.
The rise in fuel costs was **contemporary** with the demand for alternative fuels.

cynical
sin´ i kəl

adj. Doubtful of the sincerity of others' motives; skeptical.
People become **cynical** about diet programs when lost weight is soon regained.

cynic *n.*
Even though many clients have lied to her, Katharine, a public defender, has not become a **cynic.**

despot
des´ pət

n. A ruler with absolute power or tyrannical control over a group of people.
In the late 1970s and early 1980s, thousands fled Haiti seeking refuge from the **despot** Jean Claude Duvalier.

despotic *adj.*
The Declaration of Independence of the United States asserts the government's right to overthrow a **despotic** ruler.

enunciate
ə nun´ sē āt´

v. 1. To pronounce clearly.
In speech class we learn to **enunciate** our words.

2. To state; to announce.
The president **enunciated** his objectives for the coming year in his State of the Union address to Congress.

impediment
im ped´ ə mənt

n. Anything that gets in the way; an obstacle.
After the hurricane, fallen trees were **impediments** to traffic in our neighborhood.

impoverish
im päv´ ər ish

v. 1. To make poor.
Uncontrolled gambling can **impoverish** a person.

2. To take away.
Continual overfarming **impoverishes** the soil.

impoverished *adj.*
The Peace Corps is an agency of the United States government that sends volunteers to improve living standards in **impoverished** areas of the world.

indolent in´ də lənt	*adj.* Indulging in ease; avoiding exertion; lazy. Being in the torrid heat of the tropical sun makes one feel **indolent.** **indolence** *n.* His failure to reach his goal certainly cannot be attributed to **indolence.**
sagacious sə gā´ shəs	*adj.* Showing sound judgment; wise. My grandmother's **sagacious** advice has guided me many times over the years. **sagacity** *n.* I was amazed when she questioned the **sagacity** of my plan to climb the mountain.
secular sek´ yə lər	*adj.* Worldly; not connected with a church or religion. The choir included a few **secular** songs in the memorial service.
speculate spek´ yo͞o lāt´	*v.* 1. To think about or make guesses. As we waited, we **speculated** about whether he'd keep his promise and show up. 2. To engage in a risky business venture. She lost a great deal of money when she **speculated** in the stock market last year.
strife strīf	*n.* Conflict or struggle. The **strife** between the two families has existed for a few years now.
venerate ven´ ər āt	*v.* To show great respect for. Asian cultures **venerate** their ancestors long after they have died.
voracious vô rā´ shəs	*adj.* 1. Ravenous; desiring and eating a large amount of food. We arrived back from our hike with **voracious** appetites. 2. Greatly eager. Simon has been a **voracious** reader since childhood.
wane wān	*v.* To get smaller, dimmer, or weaker; to near an end. When interest in sitcoms **waned,** the television networks switched to reality shows.

5A ▶ Understanding Meanings

Read the sentences. If a sentence correctly uses the word in bold, write *C* on the line. If a sentence is incorrect, rewrite it so that the vocabulary word in bold is used correctly.

1. A **voracious** creature is very hungry.

_____

_____

2. A **sagacious** person is difficult to rouse to action.

_____

_____

3. A **secular** group is one concerned primarily with spiritual or religious matters.

_____

_____

4. **Strife** between people is a condition of tranquility.

_____

_____

5. To **speculate** is to make a precarious monetary transaction.

_____

_____

6. A **callow** person is someone who is easily frightened.

_____

_____

7. To **venerate** someone is to hold that person in high regard.

_____

_____

8. A **despot** is a person who avoids the company of others.

_____

_____

9. **Indolence** is a state of indecision.

_____

_____

10. To **enunciate** a principle is to express it clearly.

_____

_____

11. **Contemporaries** are people living in the same area of the world.

_____

_____

12. To **wane** is to go from place to place in aimless fashion.

_____

_____

13. An **impediment** is a barrier or obstruction.

_____

_____

callow
contemporary
cynical
despot
enunciate
impediment
impoverish
indolent
sagacious
secular
speculate
strife
venerate
voracious
wane

14. A **cynic** is a person who is easily deceived.

_____

_____

15. To be **impoverished** is to lack sufficient money for one's needs.

_____

_____

5B ▶ Using Words

If the word (or a form of the word) in bold fits in a sentence in the group following it, write the word in the blank space. If the word does not fit, leave the space empty. There may be more than one correct answer.

1. **enunciate**

   (a) She has yet to _____ the concerns that are motivating her to run for a seat on the school board.

   (b) The letters were so faded that I could not _____ the message.

   (c) The child _____ her words as she read the poem to the assembly.

2. **sagacity**

   (a) Pericles, known for his _____ , made ancient Athens an early center of democracy, art, and literature in the fifth century B.C.E.

   (b) The _____ of the tennis net can be corrected simply by tightening it.

   (c) You'll be able to squeeze into this jacket because of the _____ of the fabric.

3. **wane**

   (a) Her strength did not start to _____ until she was well into her eighties.

   (b) After the moon is full, it begins to _____ .

   (c) His face was so _____ that I felt something must be the matter with him.

4. **callow**

   (a) As an intern, I produced _____ work that always had to be checked by my supervisor.

   (b) Those peaches are still too _____ to be eaten.

   (c) When I was a _____ schoolboy, I didn't have the courage to speak my mind.

5. **impoverish**

    (a) The farmers were _____ by a series of poor harvests.

    (b) Cars and trucks abandoned by the side of the road _____ the highway.

    (c) Determined that her children not be culturally _____ , she took them frequently to the library.

6. **speculate**

    (a) I'm not prepared to _____ about what happened to them after they left here.

    (b) Can you prove that they _____ with the money entrusted to their safekeeping?

    (c) I _____ the facts for the group in order to help them reach a decision.

7. **strife**

    (a) Our math teacher said that we must _____ to do better on our next quiz.

    (b) "Jealousy and greed cause much _____ in the world," she sighed.

    (c) Frequent _____ between labor and management in the factory resulted in many work stoppages.

8. **contemporary**

    (a) Advances in biomedical research are _____ with a growing interest in alternative medicine.

    (b) Sally Ride and Judith Resnik, the first and second women astronauts, were

    _____ .

    (c) This is just a _____ arrangement until we come up with something better.

callow
contemporary
cynical
despot
enunciate
impediment
impoverish
indolent
sagacious
secular
speculate
strife
venerate
voracious
wane

Fill in the missing word in each of the sentences. Then write a brief definition of the word. The number in parenthesis shows the lesson in which the word appears.

1. The prefix *con-* means "with." It combines with the Latin *tempus* (time) to form the English word _____ (5).

   Definition: _____

2. The prefix *ex-* means "from" or "out." It combines with the Latin *tollere* (to lift) to form the English word _____ (1).

   Definition: _____

3. The prefix *inter-* means "between." It combines with the Latin *mittere* (to send) to form the English word _____ (1).

   Definition: _____

4. The prefix *in-* means "not." It combines with the Latin *superare* (to overcome) to form the English word _____ (1).

   Definition: _____

5. The same prefix combines with the Latin *dolare* (to feel pain) to form the English word _____ (5).

   Definition: _____

6. The Latin *vagus* means "wandering." It forms the English word _____ (1).

   Definition: _____

7. The prefix *de-* means "from." It combines with the Latin *trahere* (to draw; to pull) to form the English word _____ (1).

   Definition: _____

8. The Latin *vorare* means "to devour." It forms the English word _____ (5).

   Definition: _____

9. The Latin *torrere* means "to parch." It forms the English word _____ (2).

   Definition: _____

10. The Latin *visus* means "appearance." It forms the English word _____ (1).

    Definition: _____

Circle the letter of each sentence that suggests the numbered bold vocabulary word. In each group, you may circle more than one letter or none at all.

1. **indolence**
   (a) We didn't have to lift a finger the whole time we were there.
   (b) Mr. Badger opened one eye. "Go away," he said and resumed his nap.
   (c) "Why did you slam that door as you left?" she asked critically.

2. **voracious**
   (a) "I don't think you are being truthful," asserted Isaiah.
   (b) "Take away their plates," Alice cried, "before they eat them, too!"
   (c) Simone spends all her babysitting money on science fiction.

3. **contemporary**
   (a) Listening to my friend Jody has taught me a great deal.
   (b) It will be another two years before the bridge is completed.
   (c) He was available to work for only a few months, so he did substitute teaching.

4. **venerate**
   (a) Many Indian people hold Mahatma Gandhi in high regard.
   (b) The monks bowed low before the massive statue of the reclining Buddha in Bangkok.
   (c) This ring has been in my family for four generations.

5. **cynic**
   (a) Don't pay full price for computer parts; I can get them wholesale.
   (b) "You're so egotistical," she said. "You think you're so great!"
   (c) Some people think that politicians care about just one thing: getting reelected.

6. **speculate**
   (a) Joannie told me she spends twenty dollars a week on lottery tickets.
   (b) In fifty years, gasoline-powered cars will be a thing of the past.
   (c) I expect gold to double in price within two years, so I'm buying it now.

7. **despot**
   (a) The rule in our house is "If you don't eat your vegetables, you can't have any dessert."
   (b) "Off with his head!" was a frequent order issued by the Queen of Hearts in *Alice's Adventures in Wonderland*.
   (c) In the novel, the prince ordered every male in the kingdom to shave off his beard.

8. **secular**
   (a) Dellison is an old private school that has never been affiliated with any religious group.
   (b) Those serving on the commission were paid a dollar a year.
   (c) She hoped to be reunited with her sister.

callow
contemporary
cynical
despot
enunciate
impediment
impoverish
indolent
sagacious
secular
speculate
strife
venerate
voracious
wane

9. **impediment**

    (a) The mayor laid the foundation stone of the new hospital.

    (b) The crafts fair was held indoors this year because of the bad weather.

    (c) Not speaking the language put me at a disadvantage.

10. **enunciate**

    (a) Elocution lessons are intended to sharpen one's vocal delivery.

    (b) In the musical *My Fair Lady*, Eliza Doolittle learns to speak English with graceful clarity and impeccable grammar.

    (c) "He did it!" she cried, pointing at the trembling figure before her.

5E   Passage

Read the passage. Then answer the questions that follow it.

Ideas That Endure

The greatest educators are those whose lessons are still remembered centuries after their deaths. Among this select group, few stand higher than the Chinese sage Confucius. He was the first to **enunciate** the Golden Rule—treat others as you would have them treat you.

Confucius was born into a noble but **impoverished** family in 551 B.C.E. in what is now the province of Shantung. His father died when he was three; as a young man he worked as a herder and storekeeper in order to support himself and his widowed mother. Unable to pay for a formal education, he became a **voracious** reader whose wide and deep learning soon earned him a formidable reputation as a scholar.

Hired as a tutor to the sons of the wealthy, he decided to open his own school. A willingness to learn was the only requirement; lack of money was no **impediment** since Confucius required the wealthier parents to pay for the education of the poorer students. Many of his students went on to hold important government offices, thereby adding to his reputation as a man of learning and moral character. Almost all who knew Confucius extolled his virtues.

An exception to these admirers was Lao-tzu, a man whose writings are second only to those of Confucius in their impact on China. The two men met when Confucius was in his early thirties. Lao-tzu was more than fifty years his senior. Confucius was deeply impressed by the older man's wisdom, but Lao-tzu, **venerated** as the founder of the religion of Taoism, thought the younger man **callow.** This judgment is not surprising, for Lao-tzu's concerns were spiritual, while Confucius's thoughts were focused largely on **secular** matters. For example, Confucius declined to discuss whether the soul survives the death of the body. His position was that since one cannot understand the meaning of life, there is no point in **speculating** about the mystery of death.

Confucius's concern had always been with such practical questions as how to achieve good government and how best to conduct relations within the family and between individuals. His answer to both questions was *li*, translated as "good manners." That meant those in authority, whether in government or in the family, must show respect to those beneath them. The ideas of Confucius were particularly appropriate for his time because during that period China lacked a strong central government. **Despotic** warlords ruled China, and their constant **strife** and widespread vice brought disorder and misery to the common people. In the words of a **contemporary** of Confucius, "The world had fallen into decay, and right principles had disappeared." As a result of his ties with former pupils, Confucius was made a minister of justice in his native province of Lu. Not surprisingly, he showed himself to be a **sagacious** administrator. As a high official, Confucius was able to practice *li* and encourage others to do the same. In this way, he helped restore order in the land, all but eliminated crime, and gave the people of Lu a period of peace.

This happy state was short-lived. The ruler of Lu province grew **indolent** and began taking advice from those who wanted to return to the old days. They wanted more opportunity for personal enrichment by corrupting government officials. Confucius found his influence **waning.** After four years in office, he was dismissed as a result of the maneuvers of jealous rivals. Now fifty-six, Confucius spent the next thirteen years traveling throughout China, hoping to find a ruler who would accept his guidance. Although he failed in this endeavor, there is no evidence that he ever became **cynical.** Although Confucius did not put his principles into writing, a group of his followers passed on his teachings. These dealt with codes of conduct based on the belief that strong moral character is the basis of civilization and that inner goodness is reflected in outer behavior. Some three thousand principles of Confucius survived and became the basis of Chinese education for over two thousand years.

callow
contemporary
cynical
despot
enunciate
impediment
impoverish
indolent
sagacious
secular
speculate
strife
venerate
voracious
wane

▶ **Answer each question in the form of a sentence. If a question does not contain a word from the lesson, use one in your answer. Use each word only once.**

1. Why was Confucius not able to afford a formal education?

_____

_____

2. What details in the passage suggest that Confucius was not an **indolent** youth?

_____

_____

3. How did Confucius educate himself?

_____

_____

4. How might following the Golden Rule reduce **strife?**

_____

_____

5. What would be an appropriate description for the person who says that the Golden Rule is "The one with the gold makes the rules"?

_____

_____

6. What evidence do we have that the followers of Confucius **venerated** him?

_____

_____

7. What **impediments** did Confucius have to overcome as a young man?

_____

_____

8. What were some of the differences in point of view between Confucius and Lao-tzu?

_____

_____

9. How do you know that Confucius and Lao-tzu were **contemporaries?**

_____

_____

10. What contributed to Lao-tzu's impression that Confucius was **callow?**

_____

_____

11. What quality do Confucius and Lao-tzu share?

_____

_____

12. Why was it unlikely that **despotic** rulers would appoint Confucius to a position of authority?

_____

_____

13. Why do you think interest in Confucius' teachings has not **waned?**

_____

_____

- The adjectives **contemporary** and *contemporaneous* mean the same thing. To say that something is *contemporary* (without specifying with what) is understood to mean "*contemporary* with us," or modern. Thus, *contemporary* fashions may be contrasted with those of the 1920s.

- The Latin *dolere* means "to feel pain" and forms the root of several English words associated with suffering. In English, *dolor* means "sorrow" or "grief." (Many of the works of the American poet Emily Dickenson are filled with a spirit of *dolor*.) *Doleful* means "full of pain or sorrow." (Her *doleful* expression told me her dog was still missing.)

- One of the functions of the prefix *in-* or *im-* is to turn a word into its opposite. **Indolent** once meant "free of pain." The fact that indolent now means "lazy" or "idle" seems to suggest that activity is painful; however, since most societies believe activity to be a good thing, the word *indolent* is now considered derogatory.

callow
contemporary
cynical
despot
enunciate
impediment
impoverish
indolent
sagacious
secular
speculate
strife
venerate
voracious
wane

For more practice and games, go to **www.WordlyWise3000.com**.

| Word List | Study the definitions of the words. Then do the exercises that follow. |

apropos
ap rə pō´

adj. Fitting the occasion; suitable or apt.
The governor's red, white, and blue blouse seemed quite **apropos** for her post-election celebration.

ascendancy
ə sen´dən sē

n. Controlling influence; domination.
The **ascendancy** of the United States as a world power coincided with the decline of the British Empire.

assess
ə ses´

v. To analyze and determine the nature, value, or importance of.
After I **assessed** the difficulties we faced in repairing the storm damage, I proposed a three-part plan.

assessment *n.*
Our **assessment** of the water quality of the bay shows that there has been a significant improvement over the last five years.

aver
ə vʉr´

v. To declare positively; to state as the truth.
The lawyer **averred** that her client was innocent.

concede
kən sēd´

v. 1. To admit to be true, often reluctantly.
Bungee jumpers **concede** that the sport can be dangerous.

2. To grant or let have.
When her queen was placed in an indefensible position, Marla **conceded** the chess game to her opponent.

deficient
də fish´ ənt

adj. Lacking.
A diet **deficient** in fruits and vegetables won't provide enough vitamins for good nutrition.

deficiency *n.*
Teachers argued that students experienced a serious **deficiency** when schools could not provide music and art education.

dogma
dôg´mə

n. An unproven principle or belief held to be true.
The economic theory that the wealth of large companies will trickle down to others in the society was **dogma** to many in the 1980s.

dogmatic *adj.* Overly positive and assertive about something that cannot be proved.
While we are enthusiastic about our method of teaching dance, we try not to be **dogmatic** in our approach.

embody
em bäd´ē

v. 1. To put an idea into a form that can be seen.
Picasso's great painting *Guernica* **embodies** his ideas about the barbarity of war.

2. To make part of a system; incorporate.
The Bill of Rights **embodies** the basic freedoms of all Americans.

impart
im pärt´

v. 1. To make known; disclose.
He **imparted** his views in such a humorous manner that we were unsure whether to take them seriously.

2. To bestow.
The capers **impart** just the right amount of piquancy to the fish sauce.

oratory
or´ ə tôr ē

n. The art of public speaking.
Ms. Wade's inspired **oratory** made her address the high point of the convention.

orator *n.* A public speaker.
Patrick Henry, a contemporary of George Washington, was a brilliant **orator.**

oratorical *adj.*
Attending a workshop on public speaking can help sharpen one's **oratorical** skills.

propagate
präp´ ə gāt

v. 1. To reproduce.
The scientists were puzzled when the frogs that **propagated** in the fall had unusually few offspring.

2. To cause to reproduce.
Begonias are easy plants to **propagate** by cuttings.

3. To foster the spread of.
The professor wrote several articles to **propagate** his theory explaining the causes of sudden climate change.

propagation *n.*
The **propagation** of information has been facilitated by the use of computers.

proponent
prə pō´ nənt

n. Someone who proposes or supports an idea; an advocate.
The bill passed easily since its **proponents** were in the majority.

rudimentary
rōō´ də men´ tər ē

adj. 1. Not yet fully developed; basic.
The **rudimentary** train system of the United States developed rapidly during the second half of the nineteenth century.

2. Elementary.
Juan speaks four languages perfectly and has a **rudimentary** knowledge of several others.

sojourn
sō´ jᵾrn

n. A visit or temporary stay.
Our summer **sojourn** with our cousins ended after six wonderful weeks in Puerto Rico.

v. To stay for a while.
We usually **sojourn** for a week or so at our grandparents' cabin as we make our way north.

vociferous
vō sif´ ər əs

adj. Making one's feelings known in a loud way.
The community's **vociferous** opposition to a stadium in their neighborhood led the governor to abandon the plan.

Read the sentences. If a sentence correctly uses the word in bold, write C on the line. If a sentence is incorrect, rewrite it so that the vocabulary word in bold is used correctly.

1. To **impart** something is to have an effect on it.

   _____

   _____

2. To **propagate** is to increase by producing offspring.

   _____

   _____

3. **Oratory** is the cultivation of fruits and vegetables.

   _____

   _____

4. A **dogma** is a brief, usually witty, saying.

   _____

   _____

5. To be in the **ascendancy** is to have power or influence.

   _____

   _____

6. To **concede** something is to hide it.

   _____

   _____

7. A **rudimentary** plan is one that is not expressed politely.

   _____

   _____

8. If a remark is **apropos,** it fits the situation perfectly.

   _____

   _____

9. To **assess** damage is to escape responsibility for it.

   _____

   _____

10. To be **deficient** is to be without certain things.

    _____

    _____

11. To **embody** a principle is to add details that may not be true.

    _____

    _____

12. A **proponent** of a scheme is one who is in favor of it.

_____

_____

13. To **sojourn** is to go on a long journey.

_____

_____

14. A **vociferous** supporter is one who cannot be trusted.

_____

_____

15. To **aver** something is to deny it happened.

_____

_____

6B Using Words

If the word (or a form of the word) in bold fits in a sentence in the group following it, write the word in the blank space. If the word does not fit, leave the space empty. There may be more than one correct answer.

1. **embody**

(a) Russo attempted to _____ the document where no one could find it.

(b) The architecture of these cathedrals _____ the religious beliefs of the age.

(c) The words "My country right or wrong" _____ the senator's philosophy.

2. **concede**

(a) We have reluctantly _____ victory to the team from Brockton.

(b) I refuse to _____ that I made an error in my calculations.

(c) Each of us _____ a quart of water after the game.

3. **ascendancy**

(a) By 49 B.C.E., Rome's _____ over the Gaulish tribes was complete.

(b) My first _____ in a hot-air balloon was a thrilling experience.

(c) The _____ of Mount Whitmore took us almost three hours.

apropos

ascendancy

assess

aver

concede

deficient

dogma

embody

impart

oratory

propagate

proponent

rudimentary

sojourn

vociferous

4. **vociferous**

    (a) The painter's early works are noted for their _____ use of color.

    (b) A _____ crowd gathered outside city hall demanding to see the mayor.

    (c) My cousin Tom is known for his _____ appetite.

5. **apropos**

    (a) What is the _____ of your paper?

    (b) For a vegetarian picnic, soyburgers would be _____ .

    (c) Greed is an _____ title for this book on how to get rich quick.

6. **rudimentary**

    (a) Luz fashioned a _____ fishing rod out of a long branch she found on the ground.

    (b) It was very _____ of you to tell Mrs. Longworth that she was gaining weight.

    (c) Ken's knowledge of cooking is so _____ he can barely boil an egg.

7. **dogma**

    (a) Try to be a little more _____ when you talk to the principal.

    (b) Carla is so _____ that I don't enjoy conversing with her.

    (c) Scientific _____ asserts that water is made up of oxygen and hydrogen.

8. **deficient**

    (a) The thermometer shows a _____ temperature, so wear a warm coat.

    (b) Bruce has shown many times that he is _____ in good judgment.

    (c) Anemia is a medical condition caused by blood that is _____= in iron.

Each group of words contains two words that are either synonyms or antonyms. Circle them. Then circle _S_ if they are synonyms or _A_ if they are antonyms.

1. noisy   rudimentary   vociferous   sedentary   S   A

2. impart   assist   withold   assess   S   A

3. evaluate   assess   enunciate   embody   S   A

4. increase   venerate   wane   regale   S   A

5. secular   flamboyant   trusting   cynical   S   A

6. hollow   sagacious   callow   secular   S   A

7. precise   haphazard   sedentary   voluntary   S   A

8. lament   exhort   implicate   urge   S   A

9. careful   voracious   punctilious   wry   S   A

10. deficient   temporal   lacking   pensive   S   A

apropos
ascendancy
assess
aver
concede
deficient
dogma
embody
impart
oratory
propagate
proponent
rudimentary
sojourn
vociferous

Circle the letter of each sentence that suggests the numbered bold vocabulary word. In each group, you may circle more than one letter or none at all.

1. **deficiency**
   (a) Nancy is unable to account for the missing sixty dollars.
   (b) Scurvy, a once common disease, can be cured with doses of vitamin C.
   (c) Here is the nail that caused your flat tire.

2. **aver**
   (a) Free markets are necessary for a thriving economy.
   (b) Oh, please take me with you!
   (c) Automobiles have caused significant damage to the environment in less than a century.

3. **propagation**
   (a) The Spanish imposed their religion on the conquered peoples of Mexico.
   (b) Coconuts drift for thousands of miles before taking root on island beaches.
   (c) Information is accessible on the Internet to anyone with a computer and a modem.

4. **oratorical**
   (a) And in conclusion, ladies and gentlemen, I would like to say this.
   (b) Thank you for inviting me to speak to you today on this important topic.
   (c) Do you mind if I sit next to Kelly?

5. **assessment**
   (a) The Mets' batting has deteriorated, but their bullpen remains strong.
   (b) The deal is just too risky for me to put money into.
   (c) The chances of an earthquake's happening here are a million to one.

6. **impart**
   (a) After we said goodbye at the railroad station, Marisol went straight home.
   (b) "The secret of success," he said, lowering his voice, "is hard work."
   (c) Alice is sure she caught chicken pox from her friend Marie.

7. **sojourn**
   (a) For eight years Miss Emily never set foot outside her house.
   (b) With no time to waste as we crossed the desert, we took turns driving through the night.
   (c) After a week in Nagoya, the musicians moved on to Taipei.

8. **proponent**
   (a) I see that I'm playing against last year's champion in the first round.
   (b) The distributor cap is cracked and will have to be replaced.
   (c) The policy of our company is "Haste makes waste."

9. **concede**

    (a) The car was going at least forty miles an hour in a school zone.

    (b) Caroline certainly has a very high opinion of herself.

    (c) The members are in complete agreement that they will not raise fees.

10. **rudimentary**

    (a) If you look very carefully, you can see that a tadpole does have legs.

    (b) My knowledge of math doesn't go much beyond adding and subtracting.

    (c) The first boats were probably made from hollowed-out logs.

Passage

Read the passage. Then answer the questions that follow it.

Silent World?

    Imagine living in a totally silent world, one in which no words are spoken and no sounds are heard. Would you be entirely unable to communicate with others, and therefore feel very isolated? Probably not if you could express your thoughts in a **rudimentary** manner by using simple gestures. Pointing to yourself, for example, would mean "me"; pointing to another person would mean "you."

    In 1755, Abbé Michel de l'Éspée used this idea to develop a simple language with its own vocabulary and grammar. At the school he founded in Paris, he taught people whose profound loss of hearing had left them speechless to communicate through hand and arm movements (later known as the "manual" method). During the same time period, a different system was developed in England and Germany; its **proponents** rejected the French method and favored teaching deaf people to enunciate words and to lip-read (later known as the "oral" method).

    At this time, the United States had no school for deaf people. Concerned about this **deficiency,** a group of Connecticut citizens sent Thomas Gallaudet, a young minister, to Europe in 1815 to make an **assessment** of both the manual and the oral approaches. For some reason, the people running the English school were unwilling to **impart** their teaching methods to Gallaudet; perhaps they feared he would lure away their students, depriving them of their livelihood. So Gallaudet went to France. After a lengthy **sojourn** in Paris, he returned to Connecticut to **propagate** the French method in the United States. His advocacy of the French approach might have had something to do with his treatment by the English.

    Within a year, Gallaudet had opened the first free school for the deaf, which later became the American School for the Deaf, in Hartford, Connecticut. Here, he used a system known as American Sign Language (ASL), in which signs are word-like units made with one or both hands to form obvious shapes and make distinctive movements. Spatial relations, direction, and orientation of hand movements comprise the grammar of ASL, which shares some elements with spoken English.

apropos
ascendancy
assess
aver
concede
deficient
dogma
embody
impart
oratory
propagate
proponent
rudimentary
sojourn
vociferous

Gallaudet's method caught on quickly; other schools opened, and for the next few decades ASL held the **ascendancy** in the United States.

Then in the 1840s, the alternative (oral) method, using actual speech and lip-reading, was introduced at the Clarke School for the Deaf in Worcester, Massachusetts. Both methods, and the different approaches they **embody,** have continued to generate **vociferous** debate. Opponents of the speech/lip-reading method claim that students who have never heard speech cannot duplicate it well enough to be understood properly. Also, lip-reading can be misleading: the lip movements when pronouncing the words *mat, bat,* and *pat,* for example, all look the same. Opponents of ASL, on the other hand, **aver** that deaf students who communicate with gestures can do so only among themselves and are thus cut off from contact with the rest of the population.

In 1969, a large residential school in Maryland introduced the concept of total communication. This philosophy, increasingly influential today, does not follow a single approach **dogmatically;** instead, it uses a combination of whatever works for a particular individual. Options include speech, lip-reading, signing, mime, gestures, finger spelling, art, reading, writing, and use of electronic media.

Since the mid-twentieth century, significant gain has been made in removing the barriers that separate people with disabilities from the rest of the population. Progress toward this end continues with the passing of federal and state legislation, the advocacy of parents and educators, and the challenges of individual citizens. One such challenge was made by Shannon Merriman, who in 1992 was a sixteen-year-old Rhode Island high school student. At that time, she tried to enter the high school Voice of Democracy contest, a national **oratorical** competition, which attracts over 200,000 entrants annually.

Merriman, having lost her hearing when she was two, communicates through ASL. When the sponsors of the competition rejected her application, she challenged the legality of their act, causing them to **concede** her the right to participate. She didn't win the competition, but she opened up one more opportunity for hearing-impaired people to participate in mainstream American life. The topic of the contest that year was particularly **apropos;** it was "My Voice in America's Future."

▶ **Answer each question in the form of a sentence. If a question does not contain a word from the lesson, use one in your answer. Use each word only once.**

1. Why would it be inaccurate to describe the education for hearing-impaired people in the United States before 1815 as **rudimentary?**

   _____

   _____

2. How do you know that Gallaudet's **sojourn** in France was successful?

   _____

   _____

3. Why did Gallaudet become a **proponent** of the method taught in France?

_____

_____

4. How was Gallaudet's reception in France different from that in England?

_____

_____

5. As a means of communication, does American Sign Language have any **deficiencies,** in your opinion?

_____

_____

6. Why was American Sign Language in the **ascendancy** after it was introduced in the U.S.?

_____

_____

7. What is a problem with lip-reading that supporters of the oral method might **concede?**

_____

_____

8. Why do you think the debate over the competing methods was **vociferous** at times?

_____

_____

9. How is the total communication approach related to American Sign Language and lip-reading?

_____

_____

apropos

ascendancy

assess

aver

concede

deficient

dogma

embody

impart

oratory

propagate

proponent

rudimentary

sojourn

vociferous

10. Why would it be inaccurate to describe the total communication approach as **dogmatic?**

_____

_____

11. Describe Merriman's **assessment** of the rejection of her application to enter the Voice of Democracy contest.

_____

_____

12. Why was the topic of the contest so **apropos** for Merriman?

_____

_____

13. Why do you think Merriman **averred** that she had a right to compete in the contest?

_____

_____

14. How did Merriman expand the meaning of the word *oratory?*

_____

_____

FUN & FASCINATING FACTS

- The Latin word *verus,* meaning "true," forms the root of several English words. To question the *veracity* of a statement is to question its truthfulness. When one speaks of "eternal *verities,*" one is referring to truths that continue to be true for all time. A *verdict* is a decision, especially one by a jury as to guilt or innocence, that is believed to be true. To *verify* something is to establish that it is true. Finally, to **aver** something is to declare it firmly, believing strongly in its truth.

- The Latin *vox* means "voice" and is combined with the Latin word *ferre,* "to carry," to form **vociferous.** Because a *vociferous* speech is one made in a loud voice, it carries for some distance.

Lesson 7

Word List

Study the definitions of the words. Then do the exercises that follow.

amorous
am´ ər əs

adj. Expressing love or the state of being in love.
The couple exchanged **amorous** glances as they sat across from each other at the dinner table.

belittle
bē lit´ l

v. To present or speak of as unimportant or of little value.
"Why do you always try to make your efforts seem more important by **belittling** mine?" she complained.

censure
sen´ shər

v. To blame or find fault with.
The judge **censured** the lawyer for failing to file the papers on time.

n. A severe criticism or harsh judgment.
A hundred years ago, people who divorced experienced much greater **censure** than they do today.

deem
dēm

v. To consider; to believe.
Hearing about the train derailment, the mayor **deemed** it prudent to call up emergency crews from neighboring counties.

divulge
də vulj´

v. To make known something secret; to reveal.
Blackbeard **divulged** the location of the buried treasure to no one.

exorbitant
eg zôr´ bi tənt

adj. Exceeding normal bounds; greater or more than seems reasonable.
Two hundred dollars seems an **exorbitant** price for a man's shirt.

expostulate
ek späs´ chə lāt´

v. To argue earnestly in an attempt to dissuade or show strong disapproval.
My friends **expostulated** with me on the wisdom of waiting until daylight to begin my journey.

fateful
fāt´ fəl

adj. Having great or significant consequences.
The article examines President Truman's **fateful** decision to drop the atomic bomb on Hiroshima.

ingrate
in´ grāt

n. An ungrateful person.
Hanging up the phone, I felt like an **ingrate** for forgetting to thank my mother for carrying in the food and drink for my party.

injunction
in juŋk´ shən

n. 1. An order or command.
When the hurricane warning was announced, my family wisely heeded the **injunction** to evacuate the island.

2. A court order prohibiting someone from doing something.
The **injunction** stated that the company could not hire permanent replacement workers during the strike.

| **moribund** | *adj.* Close to death; in a dying state. |
| môr´ i bund´ | It is incontrovertible that the company was **moribund** when we took it over last year. |

motif	*n.* 1. A theme or idea in a work of art or literature that is developed or repeated.
mō tēf´	Throughout the novel, the author explores the **motif** of separation.
	2. A figure or design repeated in the decoration of something, such as a building or textile.
	The wallpaper for the nursery had a rabbit **motif.**

subsidize	*v.* To support by giving financial aid.
sub´ sə dīz	The government has **subsidized** countless arts projects, allowing thousands of people to enjoy music, dance, and theater in their hometowns.
	subsidy *n.* A grant of money, often provided by a government to a group or individual.
	Thanks to this **subsidy,** our dance company will be able to perform throughout the state.

| **sumptuous** | *adj.* Extravagantly splendid or costly; luxurious. |
| sump´ choo əs | After the wedding we enjoyed a **sumptuous** meal in the hotel dining room. |

| **voluble** | *adj.* Characterized by a ready flow of words; talkative. |
| vol´ yoo bəl | The **voluble** host scarcely gave his guests a chance to speak. |

7A ▶ Understanding Meanings

Read the sentences. If a sentence correctly uses the word in bold, write *C* on the line. If a sentence is incorrect, rewrite it so that the vocabulary word in bold is used correctly.

1. To **expostulate** is to become confused or perplexed.

   _____

   _____

2. A **motif** is a reason for doing something.

   _____

   _____

3. To **belittle** something is to claim it is less important than it seems.

   _____

   _____

4. To **subsidize** something is to pay some or all of the cost of it.

   _____

   _____

5. A **sumptuous** villa is one on which no expense has been spared.

_____

_____

6. To feel **amorous** is to have thoughts of love.

_____

7. An **ingrate** is a person who is not famous.

_____

8. To **divulge** something is to draw its attention elsewhere.

_____

9. A **moribund** organization is one that is not open to outsiders.

_____

10. To **censure** someone is to deny that person the right to speak.

_____

11. A **voluble** person is one who is large in size.

_____

12. To **deem** something impossible is to think that it is so.

_____

13. A **fateful** event is one that is momentous.

_____

14. An **injunction** is forcing a fluid into the body for medical purposes.

_____

15. An **exorbitant** demand is one that is greater than seems reasonable.

_____

_____

amorous
belittle
censure
deem
divulge
exorbitant
expostulate
fateful
ingrate
injunction
moribund
motif
subsidize
sumptuous
voluble

If the word (or a form of the word) in bold fits in a sentence in the group following it, write the word in the blank space. If the word does not fit, leave the space empty. There may be more than one correct answer.

1. **moribund**

    (a) The patient, although _____ , was in no pain.

    (b) Two aspirin did nothing to relieve my _____ headache.

    (c) Through gross mismanagement, the organization is now _____ .

2. **divulge**

    (a) Suzanne and Sam made me promise not to _____ their marriage plans.

    (b) At the stoplight, the street _____ into a boulevard.

    (c) Joe lifted the lid of the carved box to _____ its surprising contents.

3. **subsidize**

    (a) It was four days before the floodwaters began to _____ .

    (b) The debate was over whether the taxpayers should _____ the giant automaker.

    (c) If I _____ you the money, will you promise to repay me?

4. **deem**

    (a) You can accompany the children to the bus stop if you _____ it necessary.

    (b) That model has been _____ obsolete because this year's version outperforms it.

    (c) Why not _____ this coupon for the thirty percent discount it offers?

5. **amorous**

    (a) The soft lights and sweet music put us in an _____ mood.

    (b) The swans on the lake entwined their necks in _____ play.

    (c) The sonnets are the _____ outpourings of the poet's feelings for his wife.

6. **expostulate**

    (a) "I want nothing more to do with you," she _____ .

    (b) "We have _____ too much time already on this problem," he declared.

    (c) Jones _____ the situation to the students in a calm, methodical manner.

7. **voluble**

(a) The most _____ documents were kept in a safe deposit box at the bank.

(b) The music was so _____ that we had to shout in order to be heard.

(c) Having a conversation with such a _____ person is impossible.

8. **sumptuous**

(a) What I remember most distinctly from the photographs are the _____ furnishings of the castle's bedrooms.

(b) The stage sets for the new musical are the most _____ I have ever seen.

(c) Jonah's boss promised him a _____ raise if he continued to do well.

7c ▷ Word Study

Complete the analogies by selecting the pair of words whose relationship most resembles the relationship of the pair in capital letters. Circle the letter in front of the pair you choose.

1. VOLUBLE : SPEECH ::
   (a) painful : injury
   (b) blurry : vision
   (c) visible : eye
   (d) flamboyant : dress

2. ORATOR : WORDS ::
   (a) despot : subjects
   (b) house : bricks
   (c) pomp : parades
   (d) musician : notes

3. PROPONENT : EXTOL ::
   (a) information : impart
   (b) sojourn : remain
   (c) defeat : concede
   (d) opponent : belittle

4. INGRATE : GRATITUDE ::
   (a) gambler : luck
   (b) miser : money
   (c) invalid : health
   (d) motif : pattern

5. STRIFE : HARMONY ::
   (a) despot : fear
   (b) alacrity : speed
   (c) adage : maxim
   (d) pomp : simplicity

6. SAGACITY : MIND ::
   (a) emancipation : freedom
   (b) strength : muscle
   (c) encumbrance : burden
   (d) destitution : poverty

7. REASONABLE : EXORBITANT ::
   (a) lacking : deficient
   (b) simple : flamboyant
   (c) sagacious : wise
   (d) healthy : vibrant

amorous
belittle
censure
deem
divulge
exorbitant
expostulate
fateful
ingrate
injunction
moribund
motif
subsidize
sumptuous
voluble

8. CALLOW : MATURITY ::
   (a) laggard : impetus
   (b) voluble : voice
   (c) sumptuous : display
   (d) amorous : love

9. SPARTAN : COMFORT ::
   (a) fateful : chance
   (b) exorbitant : price
   (c) deficient : lack
   (d) destitute : money

10. HUMBLE : SUMPTUOUS ::
    (a) cynical : skeptical
    (b) voracious : ravenous
    (c) uncertain : dogmatic
    (d) thoughtful : pensive

7D   Images of Words

Circle the letter of each sentence that suggests the numbered bold vocabulary word. In each group, you may circle more than one letter or none at all.

1. **ingrate**

   (a) By excessive flattery, Simon won the confidence of Mrs. Dalloway.

   (b) After all Rosa did for Jacob, she never got so much as a thank-you.

   (c) The pitch was an easy one, and Hank drove the ball into the bleachers.

2. **belittle**

   (a) The Bulldogs came into the game unbeaten, but we cut them down to size.

   (b) "You got an *A* on that report only because Mom helped you," my brother hissed.

   (c) The original test had fifty questions, but the new version has only thirty.

3. **fateful**

   (a) General Lee's decision to charge the Union center at Gettysburg cost him dearly.

   (b) The sinking of the *Lusitania* brought the United States into World War I.

   (c) We met by chance on a flight to Chicago and were married a year later.

4. **exorbitant**

   (a) The space probe left Earth's orbit and headed for Mars.

   (b) All week, I've been sleeping twelve to fourteen hours a night.

   (c) I can't believe you paid two dollars for just one grapefruit.

5. **censure**

   (a) All letters sent from the war zone were opened and read.

   (b) It was wrong to answer your grandmother so belligerently.

   (c) The population of the United States is counted every ten years.

6. **amorous**

   (a) He used the money entrusted to his care to buy an expensive car for himself.

   (b) The amoeba is a one-celled animal that lacks a definite shape.

   (c) They have not spoken to each other since they quarreled a year ago.

7. **subsidy**

    (a) The Fulbright scholarship made it possible for Keisha to study abroad.

    (b) Government money helps keep tobacco growers in business.

    (c) My parents let me use their car whenever I come to visit.

8. **motif**

    (a) What possible reason could she have had for doing such a thing?

    (b) Carved roses figure prominently in the woodwork around the fireplaces.

    (c) The search for lost or stolen treasure is a theme that appears often in world folk tales.

9. **expostulate**

    (a) Can't you see that smoking cigarettes is foolish as well as harmful?

    (b) I urge you again to reconsider your decision to stop taking piano lessons.

    (c) Roberts slowly repeated his description of how the engine worked.

10. **injunction**

    (a) The company threatened to disobey the order to stop cutting down trees.

    (b) The mayor refused to allow the students to enter the school in spite of the judge's order.

    (c) There is a leak where the two pipes come together.

7E Passage

Read the passage. Then answer the questions that follow it.

Artists and Soulmates

amorous
belittle
censure
deem
divulge
exorbitant
expostulate
fateful
ingrate
injunction
moribund
motif
subsidize
sumptuous
voluble

    When Anita Pollitzer received a batch of charcoal drawings done by an artist friend in South Carolina, an accompanying note told her not to show them to anyone. The work was of value to the artist, but she felt the drawings had little objective merit, and she could not bear the thought of their being **belittled** by strangers. Pollitzer disagreed with her friend's assessment, so disregarding the **injunction** to keep the drawings to herself, she showed them to Alfred Stieglitz, the owner of "291," a Manhattan art gallery. The usually **voluble** Stieglitz was silent as he studied the drawings intently. Their abstract shapes, suggestive of forms in nature, were unlike anything he had seen before. Finally he looked up. "What woman did these?" he asked, for he knew instinctively that they had not been drawn by a man. Pollitzer told him they were the work of her friend Georgia O'Keeffe. "I think I will give this woman a show," Stieglitz replied.

    At the time of this **fateful** conversation in 1916, O'Keeffe was an unknown art teacher in her late twenties, while the fifty-two-year-old Stieglitz had an international reputation as a photographer and art dealer. It was almost entirely due to his efforts that photography had become recognized as one of the fine arts. *Camera Work,* his **sumptuously** printed magazine, first appeared in 1903, and his gallery at 291 Fifth Avenue, which opened two years later, sold photographic prints as works of art. An admirer of the painters Picasso and Matisse long before their work was fashionable, Stieglitz introduced these giants of modern art to the American public.

Stieglitz went ahead with his plan to give "this woman" a show without **divulging** his intention to O'Keeffe. She found out about it by accident on a visit to New York and stalked into the gallery, demanding that the drawings be taken down. Stieglitz calmly ignored her **expostulations** and told her she had no right to withhold her work from the world. The force of his conviction may have made O'Keeffe feel like an **ingrate,** for she withdrew her objection.

In the months that followed, O'Keeffe, who had moved to Texas where she was giving art lessons, was constantly in Stieglitz's thoughts. His letters to her were filled with passionate expressions of concern for her future as an artist, but his words grew increasingly **amorous** as his outpourings received a ready response. Letters passed between them at a furious rate, sometimes as many as five a day. "They knock me down," O'Keeffe wrote to Anita Pollitzer, "but I get up again."

Stieglitz was waiting to welcome O'Keeffe when she returned to New York in May 1917. The two wanted to marry, but there was one snag. Stieglitz already had a wife. The marriage was **moribund** and Stieglitz intended to get a divorce. This did not save them from the **censure** of many family members and friends who disapproved of the relationship. Stieglitz's wife came from a wealthy family, and he had used some of her money to **subsidize** his artistic ventures. These funds were cut off, and Stieglitz was reduced to accepting handouts from his brothers to survive. *Camera Work* ceased publication and his gallery closed.

The lean years ended in 1921 with a triumphant exhibition of Stieglitz's photographs; O'Keeffe had posed for forty-five of them and they created a sensation. O'Keeffe became an instant celebrity and Stieglitz was able to command the **exorbitant** sum of five thousand dollars for a single photograph of her. Two years later he arranged an exhibition of one hundred O'Keeffe paintings and drawings. Twenty sold immediately and O'Keeffe's career was launched. The next year, following his divorce, she and Stieglitz were married.

The marriage, which ended with Stieglitz's death in 1946, was marked by long separations as O'Keeffe was drawn increasingly to the American Southwest, the inspiration for much of her art. Sun-bleached skulls in desert landscapes and oversized flowers in extreme close-up are the most common **motifs** in her paintings. She outlived her husband by more than forty years, and when she died, at ninety-eight, her paintings sold for millions of dollars. Today they hang in museums and private collections throughout the United States. Her reputation continues to grow, and today she is **deemed** by most critics the greater artist of the two.

► **Answer each question in the form of a sentence. If a question does not contain a word from the lesson, use one in your answer. Use each word only once.**

1. Why is the meeting between Pollitzer and Stieglitz described as **fateful?**

   _____

   _____

2. Why might Pollitzer have had reason to fear O'Keeffe's **censure?**

   _____

   _____

3. Why was O'Keeffe taken by surprise when she saw her works exhibited?

   _____

   _____

4. Why do you think O'Keeffe **expostulated** with Stieglitz about the exhibition of her work?

   _____

   _____

5. Why is it unlikely that O'Keeffe was living in a very **sumptuous** style in Texas?

   _____

   _____

6. How did Stieglitz's **voluble** nature express itself while O'Keeffe was in Texas?

   _____

   _____

7. How did O'Keeffe respond to Stieglitz's **amorous** letters?

   _____

   _____

8. Why might Stieglitz's first wife have considered him an **ingrate?**

   _____

   _____

9. Do you think five thousand dollars is an **exorbitant** price for a photograph? Explain.

   _____

   _____

10. Why did the breakup of Stieglitz's marriage probably not come as a surprise?

    _____

    _____

11. Would you say that the **motifs** of O'Keeffe's paintings are unusual? Why or why not?

    _____

    _____

amorous
belittle
censure
deem
divulge
exorbitant
expostulate
fateful
ingrate
injunction
moribund
motif
subsidize
sumptuous
voluble

12. Why would it be inaccurate to say that O'Keeffe's paintings are **belittled** today?

_____

_____

FUN & FASCINATING FACTS

The Latin *orbita* means "track" or "course" and is the root of the word *orbit,* which means "the path of one heavenly body around another," as, for example, the moon around the earth or the planets around the sun. Combined with the prefix *ex-,* one of whose meanings is "away from," *orbita* gives us **exorbitant.** If the price of something stays within a range over a period of time and then moves off the track, showing a steep increase, the price has moved away from its accustomed course, and has become exorbitant.

Fateful and *fatal* have separate but slightly overlapping meanings. *Fateful* is the more general term, referring to that which has or could have serious consequences. *Fatal* is more specific and means "causing death" or more generally, "causing ruin." Something can be *fateful* without being *fatal*. (It was a fateful day when Rosa Parks refused to give up her seat on the Montgomery, Alabama bus.) Something can be *fatal* without being *fateful*. (A candle flame can be fatal to moths.) Something can be both *fatal* and *fateful*. An example is the maiden voyage of the *Titanic,* which sank in 1912 with the loss of over 1,500 lives.

The Latin *mori* means "to die" and forms the root of several English words. A *mortuary* is a place where dead bodies are kept before burial; a *mortal* blow is one that causes death; and to be **moribund** is to exist in a state near death. One might think that *morgue,* a synonym for *mortuary,* is formed from the same root, but this is not the case. It comes from an Old French verb, *morguer,* "to look solemnly," presumably derived from the expressions of those obliged to visit a place where cheerfulness would be inappropriate.

Lesson 8

| Word List | Study the definitions of the words. Then do the exercises that follow. |

adroit
ə droit´
adj. Clever at dealing with difficult situations; adept; skillful.
Her **adroit** handling of the boat saved us from going onto the rocks.

affront
ə frunt´
v. To insult or to offend deliberately.
There is no better way to **affront** your coworkers than to suggest that they are indolent.

n. A deliberate insult or offensive act.
We will not ignore the **affront** to our family expressed in this letter.

avocation
av ə kā´ shən
n. An activity pursued for pleasure; a hobby.
Serious artists say that painting is both their profession and their **avocation.**

crusade
krōō sād´
n. A prolonged, impassioned struggle for what is believed to be a just cause.
John Brown's **crusade** to emancipate the slaves led to his execution in 1859.

v. To engage in such a struggle.
Throughout much of his life, Ralph Nader has **crusaded** energetically to remove dangerous products from the marketplace.

definitive
də fin´ ə tiv
adj. Supplying a final answer; conclusive.
Some scholars believe that the **definitive** biography of the poet Sylvia Plath has not yet been written.

demeanor
də mēn´ ər
n. Behavior; bearing.
She must have been in shock, because her **demeanor** didn't change in the slightest as she watched her home go up in flames.

erudite
er´ yōō dīt´
adj. Having or demonstrating extensive knowledge; learned.
In her first book, the author provided an **erudite** account of the looting of artworks during World War II.

erudition *n.*
His **erudition** is evident in more than one subject.

induct
in dukt´
v. 1. To install in office, sometimes with a formal ceremony.
The president of the university was **inducted** into office in the morning and then attended a luncheon held in her honor at noon.

2. To admit to a society or to military service.
Each year the National Academy of Science **inducts** a few celebrated researchers.

induction *n.*
The **induction** ceremony into the Baseball Hall of Fame was a thrilling experience for the retired pitcher.

lapse
laps

v. 1. To fall or slip from a certain level of conduct or accomplishment.
After a month of regular exercise, we **lapsed** into inactivity.

2. To come to an end; to expire.
When the state trooper stopped me for speeding, he also discovered that my driver's license had **lapsed.**

n. 1. A minor mistake; a slip.
A **lapse** of memory caused me to miss our tennis engagement last week.

2. A pause or interval.
With such voluble students, there was never a **lapse** in class discussion.

militant
mil´ i tənt

adj. Ready to fight, especially for a cause.
My parents, **militant** supporters of public education, worked with other parents and the teachers to improve the elementary schools in our town.

n. One who is ready to fight for a cause.
Militants occupied the president's office, demanding changes in the college curriculum.

pariah
pə rī´ ə

n. A social outcast.
Her classmates treated Maria like a **pariah** when she told the principal that drugs were being sold in school.

prodigy
präd´ ə jē

n. 1. A person who shows remarkable talent at an early age.
Mozart was a musical **prodigy** who began composing at age five.

2. An amazing or extraordinary thing or event.
Everyone flocked to the new Ferris wheel, which was regarded as a **prodigy** of the age of steel.

protégé
prōt´ ə zhā

masc. n.; **protégée,** *fem. n.* One whose training or career is helped along by another.
Margaret Thatcher was a **protégée** of Edward Heath, whom she eventually replaced as British prime minister.

raucous
rô´ kəs

adj. 1. Rough and unpleasant to the ear.
The **raucous** cries of the restaurant's parrot startled the diners.

2. Boisterous and disorderly.
Before the lights went out, our camp counselor let us have a pillow fight, but made sure things didn't become too **raucous.**

tacit
tas´ it

adj. Expressed without words; implied.
You gave your **tacit** approval by not raising any objections to our plan.

Read the sentences. If a sentence correctly uses the word in bold, write *C* on the line. If a sentence is incorrect, rewrite it so that the vocabulary word in bold is used correctly.

1. A **crusade** is an Italian pastry.

   _____

   _____

2. An **induction** is a powerful explosion.

   _____

   _____

3. When an agreement **lapses,** it is no longer in effect.

   _____

   _____

4. A **prodigy** is something amazing or extraordinary.

   _____

   _____

5. An **affront** is a mistake that has serious consequences.

   _____

   _____

6. A **protégé** is a first or early version of something.

   _____

   _____

7. A **raucous** cry is one that is not very pleasant to the ear.

   _____

   _____

8. A **militant** group is one whose members wear a uniform.

   _____

   _____

9. An **erudite** person is one who is excessively proud.

   _____

   _____

10. An **avocation** is a short trip taken for pleasure.

   _____

   _____

11. One's **demeanor** is the way one behaves or presents oneself.

   _____

   _____

adroit

affront

avocation

crusade

definitive

demeanor

erudite

induct

lapse

militant

pariah

prodigy

protégé

raucous

tacit

12. An **adroit** move is one that is skillfully thought out and executed.

_____

_____

13. A **pariah** is a leader of a political, religious, or social group.

_____

_____

14. A **tacit** agreement is one that is understood but unspoken.

_____

_____

15. A **definitive** result is one that cannot reasonably be questioned.

_____

_____

8B ▶ Using Words

If the word (or a form of the word) in bold fits in a sentence in the group following it, write the word in the blank space. If the word does not fit, leave the space empty. There may be more than one correct answer.

1. **induct**

    (a) Max is taking care of some last-minute details before he is _____ into the army.

    (b) A secretary _____ me across the hall and into the manager's office.

    (c) Ty Cobb was the first person _____ into the Baseball Hall of Fame.

2. **militant**

    (a) As the peasants became more _____ , the soldiers became more violent.

    (b) We belong to an organization that has become more _____ in protecting the environment.

    (c) Colonel and brigadier general are senior _____ ranks.

3. **crusade**

    (a) Senator Braun's _____ for the White House was starting to falter.

    (b) The government's _____ against drunk drivers began having an effect in the 1980s.

    (c) Those who _____ against unnecessary violence in movies deserve our support.

4. **lapse**

   (a) I'm afraid he will _____ into his old bad habits if he doesn't get help.

   (b) Don't allow your passport to _____ if you are going abroad this year.

   (c) A single C+ is his only _____ in an otherwise perfect record of straight As.

5. **raucous**

   (a) The coach's voice was _____ from shouting at the rookie players throughout practice.

   (b) The _____ weekend parties at Wetherby House disturb the entire neighborhood.

   (c) The wound had been left unattended and was now _____ and inflamed.

6. **protégé**

   (a) Being a _____ of a Supreme Court Justice greatly helped her legal career.

   (b) As an endangered species, the manatee has _____ status.

   (c) My cousin was a chess _____ .

7. **adroit**

   (a) Her _____ replies to reporters' tough questions earned her their respect.

   (b) He gave me an _____ look when I asked him what help he needed.

   (c) The sheepdog's _____ maneuvering kept the flock moving smoothly to the pasture.

8. **definitive**

   (a) It now seems _____ that Friday's parade will have to be canceled.

   (b) The public is entitled to _____ answers to these troubling questions.

   (c) The results of your study, while not _____ , are very significant.

adroit
affront
avocation
crusade
definitive
demeanor
erudite
induct
lapse
militant
pariah
prodigy
protégé
raucous
tacit

Choose from the two words provided and use each word only once when filling in the spaces. One space should be left blank.

adroit / skillful

1. Did you notice the _____ way she changed the subject?

2. A(n) _____ carpenter could do the work in two hours.

3. Suzie was _____ with the math problem.

erudite / clever

4. It was _____ of Jeff to change the subject whenever politics was mentioned.

5. A person familiar with the literature of eight languages can be called _____ .

6. It's _____ the way the moon always shows the same face to Earth.

censure / criticize

7. People sometimes _____ what they don't understand.

8. The United States Senate can _____ a member for unethical behavior.

9. "Don't _____ my right to free speech."

divulge / reveal

10. A close inspection was able to _____ several small surface cracks.

11. The information he planned to _____ was deliberately misleading.

12. Those actors _____ their speeches too quickly.

cynical / skeptical

13. It is smart to be _____ of claims that seem too good to be true.

14. These reports are too _____ to be believed.

15. A child may become _____ if his parents don't keep their promises.

Circle the letter of each sentence that suggests the numbered bold vocabulary word. In each group, you may circle more than one letter or none at all.

1. **avocation**
   (a) Dr. Muramoto worked as a family physician in Tate County for over forty years.
   (b) Every winter we go to the Dominican Republic for two weeks.
   (c) Jay goes horseback riding every weekend.

2. **demeanor**
   (a) Ellie claimed that having to perform menial tasks was beneath her.
   (b) Everyone agreed that Warren Harding looked every inch a president.
   (c) Her mischievous expression told us that she had planned a surprise for us.

3. **militant**
   (a) The book gives a brief history of every war fought by China.
   (b) The O'Garas demanded unquestioned obedience from their children.
   (c) Many Serbs opposed any negotiations with the Bosnians.

4. **protégé(e)**
   (a) As game warden, Mr. Seavers was responsible for a thousand acres of woodland.
   (b) The FDA is an agency set up to monitor the safety of food and drugs.
   (c) Both her coach and her mother traveled with her to the ice-skating competitions.

5. **affront**
   (a) Aaron told Cheryl to her face that she was not welcome in his home.
   (b) As the hurricane swept up the Georgia coast it caused extensive damage.
   (c) Speaking in a hostile tone, one member of the Board of Trustees repeatedly challenged the honesty of the chairperson.

6. **crusade**
   (a) On January 1, Marcy resolved to get more exercise in the coming year.
   (b) Seven marching bands took part in the Fourth of July parade.
   (c) The library will not make you pay fines for overdue books returned in May.

7. **erudition**
   (a) Dr. Blair's translation of the Old Akkadian texts won him much praise.
   (b) My short story was rejected by the magazine without an explanation.
   (c) Bertrand Russell tried to show that mathematics could be derived from logic.

8. **tacit**
   (a) Tony and Daniel exchanged glances and knew at once what they had to do.
   (b) She signaled her approval of my action by giving me a wink.
   (c) The repair person told me there would be no charge, but nothing was put in writing.

adroit
affront
avocation
crusade
definitive
demeanor
erudite
induct
lapse
militant
pariah
prodigy
protégé
raucous
tacit

9. **prodigy**

    (a) Heidi could see no way out of the predicament she now found herself in.

    (b) The Trojans stared in wonder at the enormous wooden horse at the gate.

    (c) By the age of four, Rajendra could speak several languages fluently.

10. **pariah**

    (a) When the Rogovins first moved to London, they had no friends.

    (b) No one would sit next to Tyrone in class when he was sneezing and coughing.

    (c) Gwen had lived in Paris for more than fifteen years.

8E   Passage

Read the passage. Then answer the questions that follow it.

First Gentleman of Sports

The **raucous** boxing fans, gathered at Madison Square Garden in New York on February 6, 1993, **lapsed** into silence as the announcement came over the public address system. Tennis champion Arthur Ashe had just died of pneumonia. With their response, the crowd paid their respects to a man whose presence had been felt far beyond the world of tennis. His death, though shocking, was not entirely unexpected. A year earlier, knowing that newspapers were about to reveal the fact that he was suffering from AIDS, Ashe called a news conference to announce that he had contracted the disease from infected blood he had received during heart bypass surgery in 1983.

Arthur Ashe was born in Richmond, Virginia, in 1943. When he was six, his mother died. His father, a parks policeman, was left to raise their two sons alone in a society where the races were legally segregated. Because of his father's occupation, Ashe was allowed on the whites-only city tennis courts. He began playing on these courts at the age of seven and demonstrated a natural ability for the game. At the age of ten, he met Dr. Walter Johnson, an African American physician whose **avocation** was assisting young black tennis players. "Dr. J." recognized the young boy as a tennis **prodigy** and took him under his wing. The doctor arranged for his **protégé** to attend tennis camps and to take part in competitions.

In 1955, when Ashe was thirteen, he tried to enter a tournament in his hometown of Richmond. He was rejected because of his race. This and other such **affronts** to his dignity led ultimately to his **crusade** to change the image of tennis as a white, middle-class game. His accomplishments in this area include starting tennis programs in five major cities and helping found the National Junior Tennis League. These acts were designed to open up the game to inner-city youth.

Ashe's calm **demeanor** on the tennis court earned him the respect of spectators everywhere. It was a **tacit** rebuke to his opponents, who often went out of their way to attract attention by hurling their rackets to the ground and engaging in other tantrums. However, Ashe's placid manner never fooled anyone into thinking that he lacked fire. He intimidated his opponents with the ferocity of his play; his smashing serve and **adroit** placing of the ball (he developed sixteen variations of his backhand alone) were especially feared.

In 1968, Ashe won the U.S. Open and was ranked number 1 by the United States Lawn Tennis Association. Two years later he won the Australian Open. In 1975, he reached what many consider the summit of tennis achievement by winning the men's singles title at Wimbledon. In 1980, he retired from active playing because of a heart condition, which indirectly caused his premature death. For the next five years, he captained the United States Davis Cup Team, and in 1985 he was **inducted** into the International Tennis Hall of Fame.

In his retirement, Ashe wanted to be more than a celebrity. He served as national chairman of the American Heart Association and also raised funds for AIDS research. He proved himself to be a graceful and **erudite** writer. His major work, *A Hard Road to Glory: A History of the African-American Athlete*, published in 1988, is recognized as the **definitive** work on the subject.

In his memoir *Days of Grace*, published in 1993, Ashe says, "While blood was pouring in the streets of Birmingham, Memphis, and Biloxi . . . dressed in immaculate whites, I was elegantly stroking tennis balls in perfectly paved courts in California, New York, and Europe." As if to make up for his earlier detachment from the Civil Rights Movement, Ashe became increasingly **militant** in his later years. He marched in protests against South Africa's apartheid system. He protested the policy of the United States against Haitian refugees. On these and other occasions, he was arrested. Although in his memoir he writes, "I am with Thoreau, Gandhi, and Martin Luther King in their belief that violence achieves nothing but the destruction of the individual soul and the corruption of the state," he also expresses regret that he did not see things differently earlier in life.

The state of Virginia, which had treated him and so many others of his race as **pariahs,** honored Ashe in his death. His body lay in state in Virginia's capitol in Richmond as the world mourned.

▶ **Answer each question in the form of a sentence. If a question does not contain a word from the lesson, use one in your answer. Use each word only once.**

1. How did Ashe benefit from Dr. Johnson's **avocation?**

_____

_____

2. Why did Dr. Johnson encourage and support Ashe's tennis playing?

_____

_____

adroit

affront

avocation

crusade

definitive

demeanor

erudite

induct

lapse

militant

pariah

prodigy

protégé

raucous

tacit

3. In what way was Ashe treated like a **pariah** in 1955?

_____

_____

4. Why is it likely Ashe would have been **affronted** if the newspapers had revealed he had AIDS?

_____

_____

5. What **definitive** proof is there of Ashe's paramount position in tennis?

_____

_____

6. How did Ashe's manner on the court compare to the way he played?

_____

_____

7. What is one example from the passage that shows that Ashe became more **militant** in expressing his values?

_____

_____

8. What effect did growing up in a segregated community have on Ashe's life?

_____

_____

9. What serves as an indication of Ashe's **erudition?**

_____

_____

10. Why was announcing he had AIDS an **adroit** move on Ashe's part?

_____

_____

11. What **lapse** in good medical practice led to Ashe's death? Do you think the same thing could happen today?

_____

_____

12. What purpose was served by Ashe's calm manner on the court?

_____

_____

Adroit, meaning "skillful," comes from the French phrase a *droit,* "to the right." Its antonym, *gauche* (gōsh) is unchanged in form from the French word for "left" and means "clumsy." The idea that the left side is inferior, even that there is something sinister about it, goes back to Roman times, when priests regarded signs from the left as indicators of misfortune. The word *sinister* itself comes from the Latin word for "left."

The Crusades were a series of attempts by European Christians to seize control of the Holy Land from Muslims. The first attempt took place at the end of the eleventh century; the Crusades continued for the next two hundred years. In addition to bearing arms, the Christians also carried the cross, the Latin name for which is *crux.* This gave these ventures, all of which failed, their name. Today, a **crusade** (written with a small *c*) describes any campaign waged with great energy and enthusiasm on behalf of a cause.

Historically, India has had a very rigid caste system. At the bottom were the *paraiyar,* also called "the untouchables." The British, who ruled India for several centuries, brought the word into English as **pariah,** someone who is a social outcast.

adroit

affront

avocation

crusade

definitive

demeanor

erudite

induct

lapse

militant

pariah

prodigy

protégé

raucous

tacit

Hidden Message In the boxes provided, write the words from Lessons 5 through 8 that are missing in each of the sentences. The number following each sentence gives the word list from which the missing word is taken. When the exercise is finished, the shaded boxes will spell out an observation made by the American writer H. L. Mencken (1880–1856).

1. We can only _____ as to what might happen. (5)

2. I admired the _____ way he handled the matter. (8)

3. The Tibetan people _____ the Dalai Lama. (5)

4. Don't act until you carefully _____ the situation. (6)

5. Their diet is _____ in certain vitamins. (6)

6. The government will _____ public housing. (7)

7. The young lawyer was a(n) _____ of Judge Finn. (8)

8. I was forced to _____ that I had been mistaken. (6)

9. The parrot's _____ cry of "Hello!" startled us. (8)

10. Columbus's _____ voyage took place in 1492. (7)

11. Declining membership left the society _____. (7)

12. The _____ against slavery ended in victory. (8)

13. The _____ carriage was covered in gold leaf. (7)

14. The umpire ignored the crowd's _____ protests. (6)

15. I refused to _____ the secret of my success. (6)

16. Germany's _____ began around 1870. (6)

17. The judge's _____ banned me from the property. (7)

18. A single _____ in judgment caused the tragedy. (8)

19. Such rudeness was a(n) _____ to my dignity. (8)

20. Defendants try to _____ their innocence in court. (6)

21. The engaged couple cast _____ looks at each other. (7)

22. I promised not to _____ his whereabouts. (7)

23. A series of _____ business transactions made her wealthy. (5)

24. I do not _____ it necessary for you to stay. (7)

25. In his eighties his strength began to _____. (5)

26. The accountant's _____ was birdwatching. (8)

27. Her comments, though few, are always _____. (6)

28. He made an extra effort to _____ his vowels. (5)

29. The rocket uses a(n) _____ amount of fuel. (7)

30. We will _____ the new members next week. (8)

31. Amoebas _____ by splitting in two. (6)

32. The _____ student can read Latin and Greek. (8)

33. The treaty ended the _____ between the warring groups. (5)

34. The _____ students demanded free tuition. (8)

35. He became a(n) _____, shunned by everyone. (8)

36. Her _____ showed no sign of fear. (8)

37. Don't _____ the efforts of those who tried. (7)

38. The Senate can _____ a member for just cause. (7)

39. His _____ attitude frustrated his boss. (5)

40. The rug had a flower _____ woven into it. (7)

41. The _____ imprisoned those who protested against him. (5)

42. The _____ host gave the guests no chance to talk. (7)

43. She called me a(n) _____ for forgetting to thank her. (7)

44. The monks were given no _____ duties to perform. (5)

45. Communist _____ said that capitalism was doomed. (6)

46. She had a(n) _____ appetite for detective stories. (5)

47. It is _____ to claim that most politicians are dishonest. (5)

48. The treaty must _____ basic human freedoms. (6)

49. Cries and grunts are _____ forms of speech. (6)

50. He was a(n) _____ boy, easily led astray. (5)

51. Are you a(n) _____ of the plan to raise taxes? (6)

52. We were sad when our _____ in Bali ended. (6)

53. He nodded in _____ agreement to our proposal. (8)

54. This book is the _____ work on the subject. (8)

55. This six-year-old _____ speaks ten languages. (8)

For more practice and games, go to www.WordlyWise3000.com.

| **Word List** | Study the definitions of the words. Then do the exercises that follow. |

allure
ə lŏor´

n. The power to attract or charm.
For many travelers the canals and winding streets of Venice have a particular **allure.**

antiquity
an tik´ wə tē

n. 1. The ancient world, especially before the Middle Ages.
Emperor Nero of Rome was one of the great despots of **antiquity.**

2. The quality of great age.
Only an expert can establish the **antiquity** of these jeweled brooches.

antiquities *n.* Valuable objects from ancient times.
Among the Mayan **antiquities** were several beaded masks.

appraise
ə prāz´

v. 1. To estimate the value of.
A realtor **appraised** the house across the street at $125,000.

2. To form a judgment of; to evaluate.
The foreman looked long and hard at the woman's resumé, **appraising** it carefully before offering her the job.

cleave
klēv

v. 1. To cling to or be faithful to.
Many Amish still **cleave** to their values of simplicity and self-sufficiency.

2. To split with force or a sharp instrument.
I **cleaved** a chunk of ice from the block with an ice axe.

depreciate
də prē´ shē āt´

v. 1. To make or become less in value.
Real estate in a good location can be a wise investment because it seldom **depreciates.**

2. To represent as of little value; to belittle.
Prince Charles of England **depreciates** much of contemporary architecture, preferring older, more classic designs.

facet
fas´ ət

n. 1. Any of the many small, flat surfaces on a precious stone made by cutting.
The poorly cut **facets** detract from the value of that emerald.

2. One of many sides or aspects of something.
We examined every **facet** of the scheduling problem before proposing a solution.

facsimile
fak sim´ ə lē

n. An exact copy.
"Since this document appears to be a **facsimile,** we will have to wait until I receive the original will," the lawyer said.

impervious
im pʉr´ vē əs

adj. 1. Incapable of being penetrated.
We stayed dry in the downpour because our tent is **impervious** to rain.

2. Not affected or disturbed by.
His calm demeanor as he faced the huge audience showed that he was **impervious** to stage fright, even though he'd never performed before.

nondescript nän´ di skript´	*adj.* Hard to describe because of a lack of distinctive qualities or features. Encumbered with a backpack and other paraphernalia, I walked along the endless row of **nondescript** houses looking for number 136.
quandary kwän´ də rē	*n.* A state of being in doubt about what to do. The lawyers were in a **quandary** about whether or not controversial material on the Internet is protected by the First Amendment.
repose rē pōz´	*v.* 1. To lie at rest. Until it was time to leave, I **reposed** in the hammock on the porch. 2. To place (power, etc.) in some person or group. The nation **reposes** its trust in the fairness of the federal court system. *n.* A state of rest or relaxation. Juliet's visage in **repose** was startlingly beautiful.
scintillate sint´ l āt	*v.* To flash or sparkle. The mirrors on the revolving ball suspended from the ceiling **scintillated** above the dancers. *adj.* Lively and witty. People often invited my father to dinner because his conversation was so **scintillating.**
scrutinize skro͞ot´ n īz	*v.* To examine with great care. The Internal Revenue Service inspector **scrutinized** every expenditure on my tax returns for the past four years. **scrutiny** *n.* Close examination. The detective's careful **scrutiny** of the crime scene helped uncover the solution to the mystery.
synthetic sin thet´ ik	*adj.* Not naturally produced; made by artificial processes. Most cloth today is colored with **synthetic** dyes.
transmute trans myo͞ot´	*v.* To change the form or appearance of. In the fairy tale "Rumpelstiltskin," the foolish miller claimed that his daughter could **transmute** straw into gold.

Read the sentences. If a sentence correctly uses the word in bold, write *C* on the line. If a sentence is incorrect, rewrite it so that the vocabulary word in bold is used correctly.

1. A **facsimile** is a comparison made between two similar things.

   _____

   _____

2. To be **impervious** to criticism is to be unaffected by it.

   _____

   _____

3. To **repose** is to keep changing one's position.

   _____

   _____

4. A **synthetic** substance is one whose ingredients are unknown.

   _____

   _____

5. **Antiquity** is the quality of being ancient.

   _____

   _____

6. To be **scintillating** is to be lively and witty in conversation.

   _____

   _____

7. A **facet** is a mechanism of a wheel or a bar.

   _____

   _____

allure
antiquity
appraise
cleave
depreciate
facet
facsimile
impervious
nondescript
quandary
repose
scintillate
scrutinize
synthetic
transmute

8. To **appraise** someone is to make a judgment of that person.

   _____

   _____

9. A **nondescript** person is one who has little to say.

   _____

   _____

10. To subject something to **scrutiny** is to observe it closely.

    _____

    _____

11. To **depreciate** something is to increase its value.

    _____

    _____

12. **Allure** is anything worn as an ornament or decoration.

_____

_____

13. A **quandary** is a state of uncertainty or confusion.

_____

_____

14. To **transmute** a substance is to change it into something different.

_____

_____

15. To **cleave** something is to split it.

_____

_____

9B ▶ Using Words

If the word (or a form of the word) in bold fits in a sentence in the group following it, write the word in the blank space. If the word does not fit, leave the space empty. There may be more than one correct answer.

1. **repose**

   (a) The weary traveler looked for a bench on which she might _____ her limbs.

   (b) After a night's _____ at an inn, we were once again on our way.

   (c) I am going to _____ my savings in the bank.

2. **cleave**

   (a) Notice how the new ivy tends to _____ to the exterior of the building.

   (b) We watched the sleek yacht _____ through the water.

   (c) He was determined to _____ to his principles, no matter what.

3. **transmute**

   (a) The medieval alchemists hoped they could _____ base metals into gold.

   (b) The sun is hot enough to _____ matter in the form of hydrogen into energy.

   (c) When she marries, she does not intend to _____ her name.

4. **scintillate**

    (a) The chandelier's bright lights _____ in the elegant ballroom.

    (b) He sometimes tries too hard to be _____ when he goes to parties.

    (c) She could usually _____ when something was not as it seemed.

5. **impervious**

    (a) Redwood makes good outdoor furniture because it is _____ to moisture.

    (b) The _____ weather has kept my grandmother inside for most of the winter.

    (c) A good umpire must be _____ to criticism from her team's fans.

6. **antiquity**

    (a) The _____ of these Etruscan ornaments is part of their great value.

    (b) Babylon, on the Euphrates River, was one of the great cities of _____ .

    (c) The _____ , housed in the Barnes Museum, is at least two thousand years old.

7. **allure**

    (a) A career in show business held a certain _____ for Jodie Foster from a young age.

    (b) Movie star Mae West's _____ made her a top box office draw in the 1930s.

    (c) The _____ of gold led thousands of hopeful miners to California in 1849.

8. **appraise**

    (a) It's too early to _____ the significance of the new governor's political appointments.

    (b) I would _____ his height at six feet and his weight at two hundred pounds.

    (c) Luisa is going to have the ring her great aunt left her _____ .

allure
antiquity
appraise
cleave
depreciate
facet
facsimile
impervious
nondescript
quandary
repose
scintillate
scrutinize
synthetic
transmute

Fill in the missing word in each sentence. Then write a brief definition of the word. The number in parenthesis shows the lesson in which the word appears.

1. The prefixes *im-* (not) and *per-* (through) combine with the Latin *via* (way) to form the adjective _____ (9).

   Definition: _____

2. The prefix *syn-* (together) combines with the Latin *tithenai* (to put) to form the adjective _____ (9).

   Definition: _____

3. The Latin *scintilla* (a spark) forms the verb _____ (9).

   Definition: _____

4. The prefix *trans-* (across) combines with the Latin *mutare* (to change) to form the verb _____ (9).

   Definition: _____

5. The prefix *ex-* (out of) combines with the Latin *orbita* (track; path) to form the adjective _____ (7).

   Definition: _____

6. The Latin *vox* (voice) and *ferre* (to carry) combine to form the adjective _____ (6).

   Definition: _____

7. The Latin *tacere* (to be silent) forms the adjective _____ (8).

   Definition: _____

8. The Latin *scrutari* (to search) forms the verb _____ (9).

   Definition: _____

9. The Latin *facere* (to make) and *simile* (similar) combine to form the noun _____ (9).

   Definition: _____

10. The Latin *rudus* (rough; unfinished) forms the adjective _____ (6).

    Definition: _____

Circle the letter of each sentence that suggests the numbered bold vocabulary word. In each group, you may circle more than one letter or none at all.

1. **antiquity**
   (a) Octavian, known as Augustus, became the first Roman emperor in 27 B.C.E.
   (b) At the age of 112, Minnie Ward was the oldest living person in Massachusetts.
   (c) Joanne keeps her 1955 Ford Thunderbird in showroom condition.

2. **depreciate**
   (a) The stock I bought for $1,200 was worth $600 when I sold it.
   (b) The novel, praised by critics, later became a classic.
   (c) A diet lacking in calcium causes rickets, a bone disease.

3. **nondescript**
   (a) He was difficult to describe because he looked so ordinary.
   (b) Henry cannot make up his mind about anything.
   (c) There was not a single distinctive feature about any of the new buildings in the mall.

4. **scrutiny**
   (a) When we put it under a microscope, it was clear that the $100 bill was a forgery.
   (b) Every name on the list of graduating seniors was checked for accuracy at least three times.
   (c) The customs officers looked through our luggage before our passports could be stamped.

5. **allure**
   (a) Irene stared in horrified fascination as the cobra drew back its head.
   (b) The idea of living on a tropical island holds great appeal for some people.
   (c) When he learned that the campus was close to the ski slopes, Tom decided to apply to Montana State.

6. **facet**
   (a) As she moved her hand, the diamond ring reflected light in bright flashes.
   (b) The first part of our journey took us from Chicago to Des Moines.
   (c) Raoul wasn't eager to hear his boss's lecture on punctuality again.

7. **synthetic**
   (a) Polar Fleece fabric is made in part from recycled plastic bottles.
   (b) The art historian the museum hired said the Vermeer landscape was a fake.
   (c) Saccharine is made from coal tar and is 550 times sweeter than cane sugar.

8. **quandary**
   (a) A magnificent beech tree grew at each of the town square's four corners.
   (b) I didn't know whether to sell my car or have it repaired and keep it.
   (c) I'm trying not to eat red meat, but I can't decide whether or not to include chicken in my diet.

allure
antiquity
appraise
cleave
depreciate
facet
facsimile
impervious
nondescript
quandary
repose
scintillate
scrutinize
synthetic
transmute

9. **impervious**

  (a) Bullets just bounced off Superman, the Man of Steel.

  (b) As her alarm sounded in the morning, Anita slept soundly.

  (c) Lead sheeting protects the body against radiation.

10. **facsimile**

  (a) She smiled, but it was obvious to me that it was not sincere.

  (b) It looks like a first edition of William Blake's poems, but it was printed recently.

  (c) Looking at the two documents, it's impossible to say which is the original.

9E ▶ Passage

Read the passage. Then answer the questions that follow it.

Diamonds

A diamond is the hardest substance found on Earth. It can be scratched only by another diamond and is **impervious** to even the strongest acids. A diamond is so dense that light passing through it slows to one-third its normal speed.

A diamond is a mineral form of carbon. For carbon to crystallize into a diamond, extreme heat and great pressure are required. Diamonds are likely formed in molten rock deep in the earth and then forced upward. In its natural state, a diamond can have one of several appearances, including that of a lusterless opaque gray or black stone or even a **nondescript** bit of glass.

What transforms a diamond from its natural state into the **scintillating** gem in the jeweler's display case? It depends largely on the diamond cutter's skill in cutting, sawing, and polishing. In the past, after **scrutinizing** the diamond from every angle, the cutter would **cleave** it with a single blow aimed at a precise spot, a nerve-wracking experience since the stone could shatter if struck at the wrong angle. Today, most diamonds are cut with saws that are actually thin, metal disks. Polishing, the final step in diamond cutting, requires a revolving iron wheel to create **facets**—the flat surfaces that reflect light, making the diamond sparkle. Though diamond cutting may reduce the size of the original stone by as much as fifty percent, the end result is a brilliant diamond with special **allure** and value.

Valued since **antiquity,** diamonds originally were thought to come only from India, but in the 1700s they were discovered in Brazil; in the 1800s, South Africa became a major source. Now diamonds can be found in other parts of Africa, Australia, and the United States as well.

The heaviest rough, or uncut, diamond on record was discovered in South Africa in 1905. Weighing 3,106 carats, or slightly over one and one-third pounds, it was cut the old-fashioned way. Its owner must have **reposed** great trust in the cutter, who reportedly fainted and had to be lifted off the floor after successfully completing the operation. Ultimately, this stone, the Cullinan, was cut into nine large and ninety-six smaller gems. The largest of these, the Star of Africa, weighing 530.2 carats, was presented by the South African government of Transvaal to the king of Great Britain. It is the second-largest cut diamond in the world and is kept under tight security in the Tower of London, where it forms part of the British crown jewels.

There was great excitement in the diamond world when an 890-carat rough diamond was found in South Africa in the early 1980s. Its owners hoped to cut it into a finished gem of at least 531 carats, making it larger than the Star of Africa. To help determine its final shape, diamond cutters made several plastic **facsimiles** cut in various ways. As the cutters proceeded, they realized the truth of the gem cutters' old saying: "The diamond, not the diamond cutter, tells the saw where to cut," for the owners found themselves in a **quandary:** either their diamond could be the largest in the world but would not be perfect, or it could be perfect but not the largest in the world. It finally became the world's second largest diamond at just over 400 carats. It was **appraised** at twenty million dollars.

Then in 1985, startling news came out of the diamond world. The Premier Mine, in South Africa, yielded a diamond that would be named the Golden Jubilee. After being cut, it outweighed the Star of Africa by 15.37 carats. That made it the largest cut diamond in the world. The Golden Jubilee is now the key piece in the crown jewels of the Royal Thai Palace in Thailand.

Beginning in the 1890s, attempts had been made to create **synthetic** diamonds. The problem at the time was that real diamonds are formed far below the earth's surface. There was no way to duplicate those conditions in the laboratory. Then, in the 1950s, scientists succeeded in producing pressures of one and a half million pounds per square inch, and, as a result, they were able to **transmute** graphite (composed of carbon) into industrial quality diamonds. These are good for cutting other diamonds and are useful in various kinds of drills. Today, even greater pressure produces artificial diamonds of gem-like quality with weights up to one carat. One such imitation diamond is made from the mineral zircon which, when exposed to high temperatures, loses its color and takes on a great brilliance.

A first-quality diamond can cost as much as fifty thousand dollars a carat. But size is only part of the story. A diamond's value depends on what jewelers call the four Cs: cut, clarity, carats, and color. White diamonds are highly regarded, whereas stones with a yellow or brown tinge are not. Green and blue diamonds are very rare; and the extremely rare pink diamond sells for as much as a million dollars a carat! Unfortunately, for the average buyer, diamonds are a poor investment. Like automobiles, diamonds **depreciate** substantially in value as soon as they are purchased.

allure
antiquity
appraise
cleave
depreciate
facet
facsimile
impervious
nondescript
quandary
repose
scintillate
scrutinize
synthetic
transmute

▶ **Answer each question in the form of a sentence. If a question does not contain a word from the lesson, use one in your answer. Use each word only once.**

1. In the past, how could a cutter unintentionally **depreciate** a diamond's value?

_____

_____

2. What is the special **allure** of the Golden Jubilee?

_____

_____

3. Under what conditions would a diamond fail to **scintillate?**

_____

_____

4. Why could one **repose** little confidence in a diamond bought on the street?

_____

_____

5. Why would it be easy to overlook a diamond in its natural state?

_____

_____

6. If you saw the Star of Africa in a store window, what might you conclude?

_____

_____

7. What would an expert's **scrutiny** of a diamond reveal?

_____

_____

8. Why would a diamond from **antiquity** look similar to a diamond today?

_____

_____

9. What does it take to **transmute** graphite into diamonds?

_____

_____

10. How might a "diamond" made from zircon be **appraised?**

_____

_____

FUN & FASCINATING FACTS

- Don't confuse **appraise** with the similar sounding *apprise,* which means "to inform." (The owner was delighted when I *apprised* her of the fact that her house was *appraised* at two hundred thousand dollars.)

- **Cleave** has a very unusual origin. The first definition, "to cling" (from the Anglo-Saxon *cleofian*), is nearly the opposite or the antonym of the second definition, "to split" (from the Old English *cleofan*). Over time *cleofian* and *cleofan* merged to become one word, *cleave*, with two distinct meanings.

allure

antiquity

appraise

cleave

depreciate

facet

facsimile

impervious

nondescript

quandary

repose

scintillate

scrutinize

synthetic

transmute

For more practice and games, go to **www.WordlyWise3000.com**.

| Word List | Study the definitions of the words. Then do the exercises that follow. |

amputate
am´ pyōō tāt´

v. To cut off a body part, especially by surgery.
The doctor had to **amputate** the mountain climber's frostbitten toes.

aptitude
ap´ ti tōōd´

n. A natural talent.
My sister Yolanda has an **aptitude** for math that has always made me envious.

beneficiary
ben´ ə fish´ ē er´ ē

n. One who benefits or gains an advantage from something.
Impoverished families will be the **beneficiaries** of these low-rent apartments.

boon
bōōn

n. A welcome gift or blessing.
After a long dry spell, the rain was a **boon** to the Iowa farmers.

commiserate
kə miz´ ər āt

v. To feel or express sorrow or compassion for; to sympathize.
If I'm upset about something it helps me feel better if someone **commiserates** with me.

garner
gär´ nər

v. To collect or gather; to acquire or obtain.
The school committee candidate **garnered** support by going from door to door throughout the district to meet people.

gratis
grat´ əs

adj. Without payment; free of charge.
Admission to the museum is **gratis** on Mondays.

adv. The food packages students put together before Thanksgiving were offered **gratis** to families who were destitute.

incapacitate
in´ kə pas´ ə tāt´

v. To make helpless or incapable.
Keiko was **incapacitated** for six weeks while her leg was in a cast.

incapacity *n.*
Because of the **incapacity** that resulted from her car accident, Melda missed eleven days of work.

inception
in sep´ shən

n. The beginning of an action or process.
I continue to extol the visiting artist program because it has been a success from the day of its **inception.**

magnanimous
mag nan´ ə məs

adj. Generous, unselfish, or forgiving.
Nelson Mandela was too **magnanimous** to seek revenge on his persecutors.

magnanimity *n.* Quality of being above meanness or spite; generosity of spirit enabling one to bear trouble calmly.
Although he was found to have been jailed unjustly, he displayed great **magnanimity** on his release.

myriad mir´ē əd	*n.* A very large number. A **myriad** of mosquitoes swarmed around us as we traversed the swampy area. *adj.* Very many. **Myriad** beautiful tropical fish swam in the warm waters of the gulf.
practicable prak´ti kə bəl	*adj.* 1. Capable of being done; feasible. Making a community garden in that vacant lot is a **practicable** plan, but you'll have to get permission from the city first. 2. Usable. Motor boats are not **practicable** in the waters of the Florida Everglades.
remunerate rē myoo̅´ nər āt´	*v.* To pay or reward. Were you **remunerated** for the work you did for the school's used book sale or was it voluntary? **remuneration** *n.* Acting as a public defender for clients who cannot afford a lawyer does not offer great financial **remuneration.**
solicit sə lis´ it	*v.* To ask for in a formal way. Ms. Vargas came to our apartment to **solicit** contributions to her husband's campaign for attorney general. **solicitation** *n.* Although I considered their cause a good one, I could not afford to respond to their repeated **solicitations** for money.
trite trīt	*adj.* Used so much that it is no longer fresh or new. "Fresh as a daisy" is a **trite** expression, but I sometimes find myself using it anyway.

10A ▶ Understanding Meanings

Read the sentences. If a sentence correctly uses the word in bold, write *C* on the line. If a sentence is incorrect, rewrite it so that the vocabulary word in bold is used correctly.

1. To **garner** things is to patch them up and reuse them.

_____

_____

2. A **practicable** arrangement is one that will work.

_____

_____

3. To **amputate** a limb is to cut it off.

_____

_____

4. To **solicit** advice is to reject it.

_____

_____

5. To **incapacitate** someone is to emancipate that person.

_____

_____

6. A **trite** phrase is one that is brief and to the point.

_____

_____

7. A **boon** is anything that impedes progress.

_____

_____

8. To have an **aptitude** for something is to be naturally good at it.

_____

_____

9. To **commiserate** with someone is to sympathize with that person.

_____

_____

10. A **magnanimous** gesture is one that shows generosity of spirit.

_____

_____

11. To **remunerate** someone is to praise that person.

_____

_____

12. A **beneficiary** is one who seeks to do good.

_____

_____

13. To receive something **gratis** is to get it for nothing.

_____

_____

14. A **myriad** of tasks is a very large number of them.

_____

_____

15. The **inception** of something is its start or beginning.

_____

_____

If the word (or a form of the word) in bold fits in a sentence in the group following it, write the word in the blank space. If the word does not fit, leave the space empty. There may be more than one correct answer.

1. **remunerate**

    (a) Working in a fast-food restaurant does not offer much in the way of _____ .

    (b) Many of the applicants lied on their job _____ .

    (c) There is no _____ that could make up for the inconvenience.

2. **myriad**

    (a) There were a _____ of reasons why I couldn't continue with the research project.

    (b) The sudden appearance of a _____ of ants interrupted our picnic.

    (c) There is a _____ of stars in our galaxy.

3. **amputate**

    (a) After her leg was _____ , she was fitted for an artificial one and was soon learning to walk again.

    (b) The discussion had to be _____ , since the time allotted for it had run out.

    (c) Earth is _____ into two hemispheres by the equator.

4. **commiserate**

    (a) "I wish I'd never agreed to come with you," Julius _____ .

    (b) I can _____ with you because I, too, have suffered the loss of a beloved pet.

    (c) The country is _____ into four time zones.

amputate
aptitude
beneficiary
boon
commiserate
garner
gratis
incapacitate
inception
magnanimous
myriad
practicable
remunerate
solicit
trite

5. **garner**

   (a) The film _____ much publicity when it won five Academy Awards.

   (b) The kindergarten teacher _____ the children around her and read them a story from the book of fairy tales.

   (c) Apple growers in western Massachusetts _____ a bumper crop this year.

6. **practicable**

   (a) In the early sixties, NASA determined that it was _____ to put human beingson the moon.

   (b) Sybil gained _____ experience of child care by working in a nursery.

   (c) A tunnel connecting France and England has proved to be a _____ idea.

7. **solicit**

   (a) I used the telephone to _____ our new apartment.

   (b) Many non-profit organizations actively _____ contributions from the public by mail and by phone.

   (c) I received so many _____ in the mail that I couldn't answer them all.

8. **incapacitate**

   (a) Freddy was _____ for a week after he fell off the ladder.

   (b) Regular tune-ups will keep your car from becoming _____ .

   (c) Because so many people signed up, the trip was _____ .

10C ▷ Word Study

Each group of words contains two words that are either synonyms or antonyms. Circle them. Then circle *S* if they are synonyms or *A* if they are antonyms.

1. fateful	selfish	uneasy	magnanimous	S	A
2. boon	blessing	dogma	aptitude	S	A
3. garner	repose	enable	incapacitate	S	A
4. inception	quandary	lapse	termination	S	A
5. flamboyant	nondescript	brief	erudite	S	A

6. solicit	sparkle	sojourn	scintillate	S	A
7. affront	pariah	repose	compliment	S	A
8. tacit	deficient	spoken	synthetic	S	A
9. trite	raucous	sumptuous	Spartan	S	A
10. copy	myriad	facsimile	beneficiary	S	A

 10D Images of Words

Circle the letter of each sentence that suggests the numbered bold vocabulary word. In each group, you may circle more than one letter or none at all.

1. **aptitude**
   (a) After only two lessons, Celia was skiing on the intermediate slopes.
   (b) Simone says that there is no one she can play duets with.
   (c) "Math has never been a problem for me," Jake said. "No pun intended."

2. **inception**
   (a) Kimberly is excited because she starts kindergarten today.
   (b) From now on, the store will be open twenty-four hours a day, seven days a week.
   (c) The first railroad was built in 1814 and was used to haul coal.

3. **practicable**
   (a) Seth spends at least four hours a day on the basketball court.
   (b) Solar-powered cars work best where there is abundant sunshine.
   (c) Janine can repair anything around the house that needs fixing.

4. **myriad**
   (a) The largest known meteorite weighs sixty tons and hit Earth in 1920.
   (b) There are one hundred years in a century.
   (c) The new Protocar gets over eighty miles to the gallon.

5. **gratis**
   (a) Entry to the fairground is free for children eight and under.
   (b) Will you take care of the dogs if you are free on Saturday?
   (c) The prisoner was set free after serving six months in jail.

amputate
aptitude
beneficiary
boon
commiserate
garner
gratis
incapacitate
inception
magnanimous
myriad
practicable
remunerate
solicit
trite

6. **trite**

   (a) I slept like a log last night.

   (b) The police are leaving no stone unturned in their search for evidence.

   (c) "Hello, Mo," I said. "Long time no see."

7. **beneficiary**

   (a) Each of my three cousins was left a one-third share in Grandmother's house.

   (b) Ebenezer Scrooge was a man who begrudged every penny he spent.

   (c) Children owe a debt to Drs. Salk and Sabin for developing polio vaccines.

8. **commiserate**

   (a) "I know just how you feel," said Basil.

   (b) "It serves you right!" my brother whispered.

   (c) "I hate this place," she cried.

9. **magnanimity**

   (a) Ms. McCarty used her life savings of $150,000 to set up a scholarship fund.

   (b) An electric current can cause a compass needle to be deflected.

   (c) Although they are cousins, they haven't seen each other for years.

10. **boon**

   (a) I love the car's cruise control, especially on long trips.

   (b) Until he got his electric wheelchair, James found it hard to get around.

   (c) The senior center and its varied activities have made a big difference in my mother's life.

Read the passage. Then answer the questions that follow it.

Dogs with a Cause

Debbie Walrod was an athletic young Californian, a former professional model and a ballerina, until a rare blood infection resulted in **amputation** of her legs and all her fingers. She thought her prospects for leading an active life were bleak. Then, through a program called Canine Companions for Independence (CCI), Walrod was matched with Oregon, a service dog, and her life became charged with possibility. "He's my hands, my feet, my best friend," she says gratefully.

CCI was created in 1975 by Dr. Bonita Bergin. Bonita is a teacher who specialized in helping students who were physically challenged because of injury or disease. She knew that guide dogs had provided valuable help to blind people for many years, and she wondered if it would be possible to train dogs to perform the **myriad** tasks that most of us take for granted in our daily lives. Professional dog handlers were, for the most part, discouraging; they did not consider the idea **practicable.** However, Bergin did **garner** the support of health care professionals who, up until that point, had been able to do little more than **commiserate** with clients whose disabilities left them feeling helpless.

The dogs Bergin trained were supplied **gratis** to those who could not afford them. Although she worked out of her home with helpers who received little **remuneration**, costs were high, and for the first few years, there was doubt about whether the program would succeed. Bergin **solicited** contributions from the public, and thanks to the **magnanimity** of those who responded, CCI not only survived, it flourished. During the course of her work, Bergin found that young dogs were easier to train than older dogs. She also found that Labrador retrievers and golden retrievers showed a special **aptitude** for the kind of work required, so she began breeding them for this purpose.

There's a **trite** saying that "nothing succeeds like success." The phrase certainly applies to CCI, which by 2003 was running five regional centers across the country. In addition, more than a dozen similar organizations had been established. One of them is Paws with a Cause. It provided Steven Normandin with Sage, a black Labrador. Steve was diagnosed in infancy with cerebral palsy, a disease that affects muscle coordination and left him severely **incapacitated.** Trained to follow particular commands and use special straps that Steve carries, Sage opens and closes doors, turns light switches on and off, and pushes elevator buttons. She can retrieve pencils and other small objects from the floor and even knows what to do in case of fire. Hearing the command "Get help," Sage will do just that, jumping through a window if necessary.

Since its **inception** in the early 1980s. Paws with a Cause has grown rapidly and by 2008 was operating in twenty-eight states. Of special interest is its Foster Puppies Program. Volunteers take care of puppies in their homes from the time they are

amputate
aptitude
beneficiary
boon
commiserate
garner
gratis
incapacitate
inception
magnanimous
myriad
practicable
remunerate
solicit
trite

weaned until they are a year old and mature enough to begin serious training with professional dog handlers. Among the **beneficiaries** of this program are not only those who are eventually teamed up with dogs, but also those who cared for the puppies during this critical period, many of whom are children.

Organizations like CCI and Paws with a Cause are a real **boon** to people who previously found themselves outside the mainstream of daily life. They also bring out the best in those who participate in the program, either by donating their time or their money. In addition, much has been learned about dog psychology and behavior. In 1991, Dr. Bergin formalized such studies when she founded the Assistance Dog Institute. It has been a leader in research, development, education, training, and placement of assistance dogs. What's the most surprising thing Dr. Bergin has learned about dogs? She says it's the capacity of the right puppies to learn behaviors that once seemed impossible. "Their brains are like sponges, they just soak up information," she says proudly.

▶ **Answer each question in the form of a sentence. If a question does not contain a word from the lesson, use one in your answer. Use each word only once.**

1. What do Debbie Walrod and Steven Normandin have in common?

   _____

   _____

2. If a service dog organization were to **solicit** help today, what do you think the likely response would be?

   _____

   _____

3. What was the attitude of professional dog trainers toward Bergin's plan before the **inception** of CCI?

   _____

   _____

4. What was particularly **magnanimous** about the earliest workers for Bergin?

   _____

   _____

5. How is Sage a **boon** to Steven Normandin's life?

   _____

   _____

6. What would an English teacher be likely to say about the expression "You can't teach an old dog new tricks" if it were used to explain one of Bonita Bergin's discoveries?

   _____

   _____

7. What did Bonita Bergin discover about Labrador retrievers and golden retrievers?

_____

_____

8. Why might people have **commiserated** with Debbie Walrod right after her illness?

_____

_____

FUN & FASCINATING FACTS

- Two Latin words, *magnus*, "great," and *animus*, "spirit," combine to form **magnanimous.** A *magnanimous* person is one who shows greatness of spirit. Its antonym is *pusillanimous,* formed from the Latin *pusillus,* "very small," and *animus,* "spirit," which means lacking courage, cowardly.

- Two words easily confused because their meanings overlap are *practical* and **practicable.** That which is *prac-ticable* is capable of being done; that which is *practical* is capable of being done usefully and sensibly. Converting the nation's railroad tracks into bicycle paths is *practicable* (that is, it can be done); however, since the country needs railroads more than bicycle paths, it is not *practical*. Putting chains on automobile tires in wintry weather is both *practicable* (that is, it can be done) and *practical* (because it is a sensible thing to do to prevent accidents).

amputate
aptitude
beneficiary
boon
commiserate
garner
gratis
incapacitate
inception
magnanimous
myriad
practicable
remunerate
solicit
trite

Lesson 11

Word List	Study the definitions of the words. Then do the exercises that follow.

amenity
a men´ ə tē

n. 1. A feature that contributes to physical comfort.
Air conditioning is an **amenity** that many urban dwellers in the South consider essential.

2. A feature that increases the attractiveness or value of a location.
The freshwater lake on the edge of town was an **amenity** all the residents enjoyed.

amenities *n. pl.* Acts of social courtesy.
The company president did not waste time on **amenities,** but told the employees immediately how serious the sales situation was.

averse
ə vʊrs´

adj. Having a feeling of opposition or distaste.
My parents are **averse** to our watching television while we eat dinner.

aversion *n.*
Helene's **aversion** to city life led her to rent a cabin in the mountains for a year.

complacent
kəm plā´ sənt

adj. So self-satisfied that one sees no need for change; unconcerned.
"I don't need to study," was Barry's **complacent** answer when reminded of tomorrow's final test.

complacency *n.*
My sister's **complacency** about her musical ability was shaken when she was not chosen for a solo in the opera.

decompose
dē kəm pōz´

v. To decay or to break down into basic elements.
If we add these kitchen scraps to the grass cuttings, over time they will **decompose** into a rich garden mulch.

defray
də frā´

v. To supply the money for; to pay.
Our school has money in the budget to **defray** the cost of the class's trip to Plimoth Plantation.

emanate
em´ ə nāt

v. To come out from a source.
As the boys crept down the basement stairs, a low humming noise **emanated** from the furnace.

envisage
en viz´ ij

v. To picture in one's mind; to imagine something in the future.
Few of the colonists or Native Americans living in New England in the 1600s could have **envisaged** that the forests surrounding them would be gone within a few hundred years.

facetious
fə sē´ shəs

adj. Playfully or inappropriately humorous.
Linda claims she was just being **facetious** when she asked if your new ring was a prize from the bubble gum machine.

fallacy fal´ə sē	*n.* A false or mistaken idea. Uncle Walter argues that it is a **fallacy** to think that the federal government is less efficient than state governments. **fallacious** *adj.* Mayor Thompson's argument for using school vouchers is persuasive, but it's based on a **fallacious** assertion.
furor fyo͝or´ ôr	*n.* An uproar; a state of great anger or excitement. When the surprise witness for the prosecution turned out to be the best friend of the accused, the courtroom was thrown into a **furor.**
idyll ī´ dəl	*n.* An episode or experience that is calm and carefree. Our summer **idyll** ended when the boat came to take us off the island. **idyllic** *adj.* The veranda, bordered by trees and overlooking the beach, was an **idyllic** spot for our summer luncheon.
paucity pô´ sə tē	*n.* Scarcity; smallness in number or amount. The **paucity** of the harvest became very clear when we looked at the half-empty corn crib.
porous pôr´ əs	*adj.* Full of tiny holes or spaces; easily penetrated by gas or liquid. The amount of clay in the soil of our yard prevents it from being very **porous,** so rainwater often accumulates in large pools.
supersede so͞o pər sēd´	*v.* To replace; to cause to be set aside because of superiority. By the 1960s, airplanes had **superseded** ships as the most common means for long-distance travel.
tangible tan´ jə bəl	*adj.* 1. Real; able to be touched. The curator pointed to a small stamp on the bottom of the vase as **tangible** proof of its antiquity. 2. Possible to understand or realize; not vague or uncertain. A **tangible** benefit of the insurance policy is that it cannot be canceled for any reason.

11A ▶ Understanding Meanings

Read the sentences. If a sentence correctly uses the word in bold, write *C* on the line. If a sentence is incorrect, rewrite it so that the vocabulary word in bold is used correctly.

1. To **envisage** something is to have it in the mind.

_____

_____

2. A **facetious** comment is one that is made in the heat of anger.

_____

_____

3. A **porous** substance is one that flows and can be easily poured.

_____

_____

4. To **supersede** something is to take it back or recover it.

_____

_____

5. A **tangible** result is one that is certain or definite.

_____

_____

6. An **amenity** is a feud or struggle between groups or individuals.

_____

_____

7. A **paucity** of something is a shortage of it.

_____

_____

8. A **complacent** person is one who sees no room for self-improvement.

_____

_____

9. A **furor** is a person who wields absolute power.

_____

_____

10. An **aversion** is a roundabout way of doing something.

_____

_____

11. An **idyll** is a person one greatly admires.

_____

_____

12. A **fallacy** is an incorrect idea.

_____

_____

13. To **decompose** is to become upset.

_____

_____

14. To **emanate** from somewhere is to come from that place.

_____

_____

15. To **defray** the cost of something is to provide the money for it.

_____

_____

11B Using Words

If the word (or a form of the word) in bold fits in a sentence in the group following it, write the word in the blank space. If the word does not fit, leave the space empty. There may be more than one correct answer.

1. **facetious**

   (a) Mark's _____ remarks make him unpopular and impossible to take seriously.

   (b) This cream feels extremely _____ when you apply it to the skin.

   (c) Monique gave me a _____ smile as she explained the practical joke.

2. **defray**

   (a) Greg attempted to _____ the company of $10,000 by falsifying the accounts.

   (b) The state has agreed to _____ the costs of providing nursing-home care.

   (c) Did you notice that the living-room rug has begun to _____ around the edges?

3. **porous**

   (a) Sandy soil is extremely _____ , so you must water the plants frequently.

   (b) If the skin were not _____ , we would not be able to perspire.

   (c) Water becomes more _____ as it is heated, eventually becoming vapor.

4. **decompose**

   (a) Dinosaur skeletons did not _____ even after sixty million years.

   (b) Before we could repair the engine, we had to _____ it.

   (c) Animal flesh becomes odoriferous as it begins to _____ .

amenity
averse
complacent
decompose
defray
emanate
envisage
facetious
fallacy
furor
idyll
paucity
porous
supersede
tangible

5. **amenity**

   (a) We had the old _____ removed and a new one installed.

   (b) The hotel offers every _____ , including free room service and pet care.

   (c) The village's sole _____ is a general store with an attached gas station.

6. **emanate**

   (a) Most of the criticism of the company seems to _____ from employees who were fired.

   (b) The strong fragrance _____ from the honeysuckle and the roses.

   (c) When will the next train for Philadelphia _____ from track four?

7. **complacent**

   (a) With our team leading by just two points, we couldn't afford to be _____ .

   (b) Scarcely a ripple disturbed the _____ surface of the lake.

   (c) Secure in its borders and very prosperous, the country grew _____ .

8. **envisage**

   (a) Can you _____ how the various parts of the machine will fit together?

   (b) When she married Tom, Kate did not _____ having twelve children.

   (c) The sleeping child _____ a magical world.

11C Word Study

Complete the analogies by selecting the pair of words whose relationship most resembles the relationship of the pair in capital letters. Circle the letter in front of the pair you choose.

1. COMMISERATE : SYMPATHY ::
   (a) speculate : luck
   (b) venerate : respect
   (c) solicit : help
   (d) recover : health

2. AMPUTATE : LIMB ::
   (a) cut : finger
   (b) plant : tree
   (c) prune : branch
   (d) defray : cost

3. PLEASANT : IDYLLIC ::
   (a) rare : ubiquitous
   (b) distance : remote
   (c) careful : punctilious
   (d) payment : gratis

4. BENEFICIARY : RECEIVE ::
   (a) flow : emanate
   (b) secret : divulge
   (c) fallacy: believe
   (d) donor : give

5. GARNER : DISSEMINATE ::
   (a) sparkle : scintillate
   (b) envisage : emanate
   (c) decompose : repose
   (d) collect : distribute

6. TANGIBLE : TOUCH ::
   (a) solid : melt
   (b) tacit : speak
   (c) visible : see
   (d) liquid : flow

7. MYRIAD : NUMBER ::
   (a) vast : size
   (b) practicable : purpose
   (c) complacent : attitude
   (d) ancient : antiquity

8. FACET : GEM ::
   (a) weight : diamond
   (b) volume : sphere
   (c) quality : value
   (d) side : cube

9. DEPRECIATE : BELITTLE ::
   (a) censure : reward
   (b) solicit : donate
   (c) extol : praise
   (d) scorn : venerate

10. FALLACY : ERRONEOUS ::
    (a) ingrate : grateful
    (b) visage : stern
    (c) beneficiary : beneficial
    (d) cliché : trite

11D Images of Words

Circle the letter of each sentence that suggests the numbered bold vocabulary word. In each group, you may circle more than one letter or none at all.

amenity
averse
complacent
decompose
defray
emanate
envisage
facetious
fallacy
furor
idyll
paucity
porous
supersede
tangible

1. **aversion**
   (a) We took a roundabout route because the road through Bristol was closed.
   (b) When served a slice of pork roast, Nazneen refused to eat it.
   (c) I move as far away as possible from any smokers in a public place.

2. **facetious**
   (a) The coach handed his star hitter a baseball bat and said to hold it by the skinny end.
   (b) The doctor told Chuck he should exercise more regularly.
   (c) The motorbike skidded on a patch of ice and went out of control.

3. **idyll**
   (a) In the letter, Natalie describes her relaxing month at a seaside village in Maine.
   (b) Jonathan sat on a bench, watching the rest of us picking up litter.
   (c) It took four hours of difficult climbing to reach the peak of Mt. Belvedere.

4. **furor**

    (a) After their teammate was tripped, the other hockey players found it difficult to control their anger.

    (b) The company's announcement of heavy losses for the quarter sent the stock exchange into a frenzy of activity.

    (c) His legs going like pistons, Wylie broke the record for the 100-meter race.

5. **supersede**

    (a) Maria was put in charge of the assembly line's fifty workers.

    (b) Upon Queen Victoria's death, her son ascended the throne as Edward VII.

    (c) Fuel injection has made the automobile carburetor a thing of the past.

6. **envisage**

    (a) Lincoln imagined that the freed slaves could be settled outside the United States.

    (b) Lena apologized for dropping by without calling first and said she hoped she wasn't disturbing us.

    (c) In her book, the author claims that a world without war or hunger is feasible.

7. **tangible**

    (a) A letter with the defendant's fingerprints on it was introduced into evidence.

    (b) The increase in the stock price gave Anne a profit of $6,000.

    (c) Clyde's affairs were so muddled that it took a team of lawyers to sort them out.

8. **paucity**

    (a) Rhode Island, the smallest of the fifty states, has an area of 1,214 square miles.

    (b) The choir's choices are limited because it has fewer than a dozen male voices.

    (c) My blueberry muffin contained exactly four blueberries.

9. **amenities**

    (a) The meeting began with bows, handshakes, and greetings in two languages.

    (b) The dessert tray contained French pastries and other delicacies.

    (c) The hotel supplied us with fluffy terrycloth bathrobes and a variety of expensive toiletries.

10. **fallacy**

    (a) Mary accused me of cheating on the test.

    (b) There is no truth to the belief that the death penalty deters murder.

    (c) Barb mistakenly believes that Miami is the capital of Florida.

Read the passage. Then answer the questions that follow it.

"Mount Trashmore"

There was a time when we, as a society, had no need to be concerned about garbage disposal. People were more frugal and less inclined to throw away uneaten food; in addition, few commonly used items came in bottles, cans, or cardboard boxes. The small amounts of garbage that were produced in those days ended up in the town dump. Understandably, people were **averse** to living close to such places, from which unpleasant smells **emanated** and in which rats resided. Fortunately, when land was plentiful and the population was smaller than it is today, no one had to.

As the country's population grew, it produced garbage in greater and greater quantities. Packaging became more elaborate, and we became more wasteful, making it necessary to find new ways to dispose of vast amounts of garbage. We could no longer afford to be **complacent** about garbage disposal. While recycling cans, bottles, plastic containers, and paper products has helped, it takes care of only part of the problem.

One of the major changes has been the closing of the old town dumps. They are being **superseded** by large, carefully managed landfills, a hundred acres or more in size, that receive garbage from over a wide area. The world's largest landfill was located on Staten Island and served the city of New York. It took in over ten thousand tons of solid waste a day, covered three thousand acres, and rose to a height of five hundred feet. At its inception in 1948, engineers **envisaged** it would have a life of five years. When it closed in March 2001, it had lasted over fifty years. Landfills of this size require careful management. Because the ground on which they are located is usually **porous,** it is important to protect the ground water beneath it. This is accomplished by laying down a lining of strong plastic or tightly packed clay to act as a barrier. Another consideration is how to handle the methane gas that is created as organic wastes such as food scraps and leaves break down. A common solution is to collect and process this gas in order to sell it as fuel. These sales can help **defray** the cost of running the landfill.

Anyone who thinks such a landfill must be an eyesore should pay a visit to the Riverview Highlands Ski Resort, south of Detroit. This two-hundred-foot-high hill has eight slopes, including one for expert skiers, and several lifts. Local residents refer affectionately to their resort as "Mount Trashmore." There is a good reason for this. Although visitors find it hard to believe, this **idyllic** spot was once a mountain of garbage. As it grew, workers added layers of soil so that the trash remained buried. When it was complete, the hill was grassed over, and today the local residents are delighted to have such an **amenity** in their area.

Many people worry that we are running out of sites for landfills. Scientists who study the problem offer assurances that this is a **fallacy;** they say that there is no shortage of such places, nor is there likely to be in the foreseeable future.

amenity

averse

complacent

decompose

defray

emanate

envisage

facetious

fallacy

furor

idyll

paucity

porous

supersede

tangible

Nonetheless, new challenges arise periodically. In the 1980s, for example, a **furor** erupted in the press and on television over styrofoam packaging used in the fast-food industry. Those concerned about the environment claimed that this material was a major problem at landfills because it does not **decompose** over time. Fast-food company executives, anxious to protect their image as responsible citizens, responded by ordering a switch to paper products. However, some scientists think paper lasts as long as plastic.

We know so much about garbage and its disposal because of data gathered through the Garbage Project, begun at the University of Arizona in 1973. Researchers knew that there was a **paucity** of accurate information on the subject. Over the years, at various sites around the country, some 750 people attired in lab coats, rubber gloves, and surgical masks, have sifted through hundreds of thousands of pounds of garbage, separating it into two hundred different categories.

Just as ancient garbage heaps called *middens* provide archaeologists with **tangible** evidence of the daily lives of the people who made them, so landfills present researchers of the Garbage Project with valuable information about the lives and habits of today's people. Referring to themselves **facetiously** as "garbageologists," these scientists not only provide us with knowledge about the present but also enable us to plan sensibly for the future.

▶ **Answer each question in the form of a sentence. If a question does not contain a word from the lesson, use one in your answer. Use each word only once.**

1. Why were town dumps not **idyllic** spots?

_____

_____

2. What **tangible** benefit can modern landfills offer?

_____

_____

3. How is methane gas produced at landfills?

_____

_____

4. Why are town dumps much less common now than ten years ago?

_____

_____

5. How did the fast-food industry demonstrate that it was not **complacent?**

_____

_____

6. What mistaken idea do some people have regarding sites for landfills?

_____

_____

7. In the past, what would have been the likely consequence of locating a town dump near a residential area?

_____

_____

8. Why do you think there is no **paucity** of space for future landfills?

_____

_____

9. What vision did the designers of "Mount Trashmore" have for the area?

_____

_____

10. Why would an area with clay soil be a good spot for a landfill?

_____

_____

11. How do local residents refer to the Riverview Highlands Ski Resort?

_____

_____

12. Where does the data concerning landfills come from?

_____

_____

amenity

averse

complacent

decompose

defray

emanate

envisage

facetious

fallacy

furor

idyll

paucity

porous

supersede

tangible

FUN & FASCINATING FACTS

Two words sometimes confused are **averse** and *adverse*. Perhaps this is because both are adjectives, both can take the preposition *to*, and both suggest negative qualities. In addition, the spelling of these two words is almost identical. *Averse* means "unwilling" or "reluctant." *Adverse* means "unhelpful" or "harmful." (Many people are now *averse* to sunbathing because they know that ultraviolet rays have an *adverse* effect on their health.)

What a difference a prefix makes! To **decompose** is to decay; to *discompose* is to make people feel ill at ease by causing them to lose their calm. A synonym of *discompose* is *perturb*.

Lesson **12**

adversity
ad vŭr´ sə tē

n. Misfortune; hardship.
In Dickens's novels, the heroine usually triumphs over **adversity.**

cardinal
kärd´ n əl

adj. Most important; chief.
A **cardinal** rule for investors is "don't put all your eggs in one basket."

credible
kred´ i bəl

adj. Believable; reliable.
The lawyer asserted that Mickey Fawkes was not a **credible** witness because he had already changed his statement twice.

credibility *n.*
The boy's cry of "Wolf!" no longer had any **credibility** with the villagers.

empathize
em´ pə thīz

v. To show or feel understanding of another's feelings or problems.
People all over the country **empathized** with the grieving relatives of those who had died in the plane crash.

empathy *n.*
Sharon felt no **empathy** for the foolish characters in the book.

faculty
fak´ əl tē

n. 1. Any of the natural powers of the mind and body, such as sight or hearing.
Despite his eighty-five years, he retained all his **faculties.**

2. An inborn ability; a knack.
Ms. Gidley's **faculty** for languages makes her a valuable employee in our office in Warsaw, Poland.

3. All the teachers of a school.
Professor Gomez joined the university **faculty** in 1993 as a chemistry lecturer.

harrowing
her´ ō iŋ

adj. Very distressing or acutely painful.
Some of the war scenes in the movie were so **harrowing** I almost left the theater.

impair
im pâr´

v. To damage, weaken, or lessen.
Even one alcoholic drink **impairs** a person's ability to drive.

impairment *n.*
The **impairment** of her hearing developed during her illness.

infer
in fŭr´

v. To reach a conclusion through reasoning.
Because you never return my phone calls and are always too busy to do anything with me, I **infer** that you are ending our friendship.

inference *n.*
"There's just one **inference** to be drawn from the mayor's speech," the principal expostulated. "There is no money for a biology laboratory."

intuition in´ tōo ish´ ən	*n.* Knowing or sensing something without the use of reason; an insight. Following his **intuition,** Robert chose the path to the left and soon was rewarded by a glimpse of the pond he had been seeking. **intuitive** *adj.* Monica's **intuitive** decision to scrap the text of her speech and speak without notes proved to be a wise one.
manifest man´ ə fest	*adj.* Plain to see; evident. Poverty is **manifest** in many countries with large populations and limited resources. *v.* To make clear; to reveal. Depression often **manifests** itself as puzzling fatigue and apathy.
nuance nōo´ äns	*n.* A very slight change in feeling or meaning; a gradation. Juliet's violin teacher congratulated her for bringing out the **nuances** of the Schubert sonata.
pernicious pər nish´ əs	*adj.* Very destructive or harmful. Even long-term smokers are beginning to acknowledge the **pernicious** effects of smoking on health.
solace säl´ əs	*n.* Comfort or relief in sorrow or distress; consolation. Having an energetic puppy to play with gave the children **solace** after their cocker spaniel Taffy died of old age.
treatise trēt´ is	*n.* A methodically and thoroughly written discussion of a topic. Dr. Yi's **treatise** on poisonous toads garnered much praise.
vogue vōg	*n.* The popular fashion of the time; wide acceptance or favor. Beehive hairdos, while quite in **vogue** in the 1950s, are rarely seen today.

12A ▶ Understanding Meanings

Read the sentences. If a sentence correctly uses the word in bold, write C on the line. If a sentence is incorrect, rewrite it so that the vocabulary word in bold is used correctly.

1. **Adversity** is an unfair advantage over another.

   _____

   _____

2. To become **manifest** is to become obvious.

   _____

   _____

3. A **pernicious** plan is one that must be followed exactly.

_____

_____

4. A **faculty** for something is the ability to do it well.

_____

_____

5. A **credible** report is one that is widely disseminated.

_____

_____

6. **Intuition** is a strong sense of well-being.

_____

_____

7. A **cardinal** concern is one that is spiritual rather than secular.

_____

_____

8. A **nuance** is a subtle difference.

_____

_____

9. A **harrowing** journey is one that is rather uncomfortable.

_____

_____

10. To provide **solace** to someone is to make that person feel better.

_____

_____

11. A **treatise** is a signed agreement between two or more countries.

_____

_____

12. To **infer** something is to assert it without offering proof.

_____

_____

13. To **impair** something is to reduce its effectiveness.

_____

_____

14. If a style is in **vogue,** it is popular with a few people.

_____

_____

15. To **empathize** with someone is to be able to imagine yourself in that person's situation.

_____

_____

12B ▶ Using Words

If the word (or a form of the word) in bold fits in a sentence in the group following it, write the word in the blank space. If the word does not fit, leave the space empty. There may be more than one correct answer.

1. **infer**

   (a) When Luisa quit, I drew the _____ that she had been unhappy at her job.

   (b) You cannot _____ that Bernie is a coward simply because he refuses to fight.

   (c) Each _____ must follow from the facts previously established.

2. **treatise**

   (a) The _____ banning chemical weapons was signed by forty nations.

   (b) The title of the _____ is "The Formation of Polynucleotides in DNA."

   (c) The concert concluded with a Bach _____ for violin and viola.

3. **cardinal**

   (a) The _____ element in the plan is the savings that will result for the small business.

   (b) Let me go over the _____ points again before I get into the details.

   (c) What you tell me is _____ , but I still need to check a few facts again.

4. **solace**

   (a) Those in need of _____ did not turn to her in vain.

   (b) The best _____ for the flu is bed rest and lots of liquids.

   (c) This simple but eloquent poem has been a _____ to many in times of distress.

5. **empathize**

   (a) I wish to _____ the importance of getting here on time.

   (b) Only those who have suffered a similar loss can _____ with Ronald.

   (c) Please don't say anything more to _____ your brother.

adversity
cardinal
credible
empathize
faculty
harrowing
impair
infer
intuition
manifest
nuance
pernicious
solace
treatise
vogue

6. **manifest**

(a) It soon became _____ , at least to me, that the business was losing money.

(b) We _____ our talents in an extraordinary variety of ways.

(c) I could not write a _____ answer because I didn't understand the question.

7. **credible**

(a) When Jimmy told me he had scored 100 on the test, I was extremely

_____ .

(b) It is very _____ of you to help your little brother with his homework.

(c) As we learned more details, their explanation for the broken window became

_____ .

8. **faculty**

(a) His _____ for making bread led to a summer job in a bakery.

(b) The history _____ is part of the school of arts and sciences.

(c) The _____ of smell is well developed in dogs.

12c Word Study

Change each of the adjectives into a noun by changing, adding, or dropping the suffix.
Write the word in the space provided.

Adjective	Noun
1. credible	_____
2. intuitive	_____
3. averse	_____
4. complacent	_____
5. fallacious	_____
6. idyllic	_____
7. magnanimous	_____
8. erudite	_____

Change each of the verbs into a noun by changing, adding, or dropping the suffix. Write the word in the space provided.

Verb	Noun
9. empathize	_____
10. infer	_____
11. incapacitate	_____
12. remunerate	_____
13. solicit	_____
14. scrutinize	_____
15. induct	_____
16. subsidize	_____

12D Images of Words

Circle the letter of each sentence that suggests the numbered bold vocabulary word. In each group, you may circle more than one letter or none at all.

1. **credibility**
   (a) I'm sure you can believe him.
   (b) The tabloid headline said that a baby was born with a tattoo on its arm.
   (c) If you ask me any more questions, I will scream!

2. **infer**
   (a) We must ask you not to get involved in matters that don't concern you.
   (b) The capital of Ethiopia is Addis Ababa.
   (c) If A equals B, and B equals C, then A equals C.

3. **pernicious**
   (a) For years the waste water from jewelry factories poured into the bay, eventually killing all the shellfish.
   (b) I told her that her comments were very much to the point.
   (c) I don't see how what you are saying relates to what we are discussing.

4. **faculty**
   (a) The exterior of the house was equipped with a ramp for wheelchairs.
   (b) Shelley described King George III as "old, mad, blind, despised and dying."
   (c) Reasoning appears to be a quality unique to human beings.

adversity
cardinal
credible
empathize
faculty
harrowing
impair
infer
intuition
manifest
nuance
pernicious
solace
treatise
vogue

5. **vogue**

   (a) Coffee bars seem to be popping up everywhere these days.

   (b) I am tired of hearing every person, thing, and event described as "awesome."

   (c) The Florida alligator population has increased in recent years.

6. **intuition**

   (a) I bet that boy you like will ask you out.

   (b) I'm sure things will get better from now on.

   (c) Tomorrow's forecast is for occasional showers, with some sunny periods.

7. **solace**

   (a) Solar-powered cars will reduce air pollution.

   (b) A first solo flight is both exciting and nervewracking.

   (c) My health improved when I started my exercise and diet program.

8. **manifest**

   (a) The governor told reporters the news conference would be at 1:30 p.m.

   (b) Signs of spring were all around us.

   (c) Did you remember to mail the letter I gave you?

9. **empathy**

   (a) Your cards and phone calls helped me so much during my illness.

   (b) They were poorly prepared for the hurricane that was rapidly approaching.

   (c) The street was deserted except for a solitary figure hurrying home.

10. **nuance**

    (a) Stress the word "I" when you deliver the line, "I know who did it!"

    (b) As the pianist walked on stage, the audience applauded enthusiastically.

    (c) I can tell from hearing you speak that you are from Pittsburgh.

Passage

Read the passage. Then answer the questions that follow it.

A Prison Without Bars

In a puppet play for children, Sally, one of the puppets, enters and places a marble in a basket, then leaves. Moments later, Anne, the other puppet, enters, removes the marble, and hides it in a box. When the children who are watching the play are asked where Sally will look for the marble when she returns, most of them can **infer** that she will go to the basket, even though it is empty. They understand that Sally is unaware of Anne's action. However, children who are autistic usually answer that Sally will go to the box because that is where the marble is. They cannot put themselves in Sally's place; they lack the ability to understand another person's thought processes.

Mental isolation is the **cardinal** feature of autism, which affects roughly one person in a thousand; the "Sally-Anne" test is one of the methods used to detect this condition. In one form of autism, people are unable to communicate with others; those **impaired** in this way live their lives cut off from human contact. In another, milder form, people are able to develop the **faculty** of speech. They may even **manifest** extraordinary skills in some areas—memorizing the contents of a telephone directory, for example, or solving incredibly complicated mathematical problems in their head.

In 1947, Temple Grandin's parents thought they had a perfectly normal baby girl until, at six months, she began to show the first signs of this strange and incurable condition. Children normally seek **solace** from their parents when they are hurt or upset, but Temple seemed to lack this very human trait. Her body would stiffen when she was picked up, and as she got older she would struggle to get free when she was held. When she could not have her own way, she would fly into a rage. In 1950, when she was three, she still showed no signs of learning to talk. Doctors told Temple's parents that their child was autistic and that she should be put into an institution.

At that time, the study of autism was less than ten years old. Many specialists in the field believed that it was brought about by bad parenting. According to the specialists, if parents failed to satisfy a child's emotional needs, they caused the child to withdraw into her own private world. Although there was no **credible** evidence to support this view, it remained in **vogue** for years. The theory had **pernicious** effects on parents, who suffered greatly from the idea that they were bad caregivers. Not until the 1960s was this theory discredited by the discovery that autism is caused by a condition in the brain present before birth. More recent studies have revealed that this condition can also be triggered by certain childhood diseases such as German measles.

Temple Grandin was fortunate. Instead of putting her into an institution, as doctors had recommended, when she was three her parents sent her to a special school. There, in spite of the early absence of speech, Grandin was able to learn to

adversity
cardinal
credible
empathize
faculty
harrowing
impair
infer
intuition
manifest
nuance
pernicious
solace
treatise
vogue

speak and read. Scientific and technical writing appealed to her because it is literal and does not require the **intuition** necessary to enter another person's thoughts or feelings as novels and poetry do. In her autobiography, *Emergence: Labeled Autistic*, published in 1986, Temple Grandin writes about the **harrowing** childhood experience of seeming to be locked in an invisible prison. She describes how she overcame the **adversity** of her condition and eventually became a professor of animal science at Colorado State University. Her specialty is designing systems for animal management, and she is the author of a number of **treatises** on animal behavior and on autism. In addition, she is in great demand as a public speaker.

Despite creating a successful life for herself, Temple Grandin still feels cut off from other people. She says she feels like a visitor from another planet because she cannot **empathize** with people. Even natural phenomena that create strong feelings in others, such as the magnificence of a sunset or the immensity of a starry night, arouse no emotions or feelings in her. Only by carefully studying the **nuances** of human behavior and then by practicing a set of correct responses, has she learned to relate to others. She ended a recent lecture by saying, "If I could snap my fingers and no longer be autistic, I would not, because then I wouldn't be me. Autism is part of who I am."

▶ **Answer each question in the form of a sentence. If a question does not contain a word from the lesson, use one in your answer. Use each word only once.**

1. How would you respond to the statement that autism is caused by bad parenting?

_____

_____

2. What do you think might be the most **harrowing** aspect of autism for parents of autistic children?

_____

_____

3. Describe the form of autism that Grandin does not have.

_____

_____

4. How is the response of nonautistic children to the question about the puppet play different from that of autistic children?

_____

_____

5. In what way was the theory that bad parenting caused autism **pernicious?**

_____

_____

6. How did Grandin's **impairment** first **manifest** itself?

_____

_____

7. What are some details in the passage that suggest Grandin has been successful?

_____

_____

8. For how long was the theory that bad parenting caused autism popular?

_____

_____

9. In spite of her success, what is the **cardinal** feature missing from Grandin's life?

_____

_____

10. What steps has Grandin taken to overcome her lack of **intuition** regarding other people's feelings?

_____

_____

11. Why does Grandin's story offer hope to other autistic people?

_____

_____

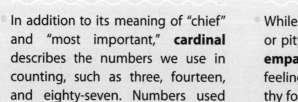

FUN & FASCINATING FACTS

adversity

cardinal

credible

empathize

faculty

harrowing

impair

infer

intuition

manifest

nuance

pernicious

solace

treatise

vogue

In addition to its meaning of "chief" and "most important," **cardinal** describes the numbers we use in counting, such as three, fourteen, and eighty-seven. Numbers used to show placement within a series, for example, third, fourteenth, and eighty-seventh, are called **ordinal** numbers.

While *sympathy* is a feeling of sorrow or pity for the sufferings of another, **empathy** is the ability to share the feelings of another. We feel sympathy for a person who has lost a loved one; when we feel empathy with a person, we are able to understand or identify with his or her emotions or experience. Both words are formed from the Greek *pathos*, meaning feeling or emotion.

Crossword Puzzle Solve the crossword puzzle by studying the clues and filling in the answer boxes. Clues followed by a number are definitions of words in Lessons 9 through 12. The number gives the word list in which the answer to the clue appears.

Clues Across

1. To come out from a source (11)
8. Plain to see; evident (12)
9. To picture in one's mind or to visualize something in the future (11)
11. Comfort or relief in sorrow or distress (12)
12. Easily penetrated by gas or liquid (11)
14. Scarcity; smallness in number or amount (11)
15. Knowing or sensing something without the use of reason (12)
16. A welcome gift or blessing (10)
18. Boxer Muhammad _____
19. Small, wolf-like prairie dog
21. The act of stealing
24. Any of the many small, flat surfaces made by cutting (9)
25. Without payment; free of charge (10)
27. To supply the money for; to pay (11)
28. To reach a conclusion through reasoning (12)
29. To collect or gather; to obtain (10)
30. Opposite of friend

Clues Down

2. Misfortune; hardship (12)
3. To change the form or appearance of (9)
4. To decay or to break down into basic elements (11)
5. To damage, weaken, or lessen (12)
6. The beginning of an action or process (10)
7. A native of Mexico
10. Delightful; enjoyable (11)
13. A natural talent (10)
17. A very slight change in feeling or meaning (12)
18. Having a feeling of opposition or distaste (11)
20. Overused and no longer fresh (10)
22. A state of great anger or excitement (11)
23. Dr. Jekyll and Mr. _____
26. _____ Arbor, home of the University of Michigan

For more practice and games, go to www.WordlyWise3000.com.

Word List	Study the definitions of the words. Then do the exercises that follow.

blandishment
blan´ dish mənt

n. (often plural) That which is intended to coax or persuade, such as flattery; an allurement.
The agent promised, among other things, to make her a star, but the actress was impervious to his **blandishments.**

deprecate
dep´ rə kāt

v. 1. To criticize or express disapproval of.
Nutritionists **deprecate** the excessive use of saturated fats in the American diet.

2. To represent as of little value.
Amy **deprecated** her own contribution to the soccer team's victory.

discomfit
dis kum´ fit

v. To make uneasy by confusing or embarrassing a person.
The reporter's questions about a bank account that showed a secret campaign fund **discomfited** the mayoral candidate.

meteoric
mēt´ ē ôr´ ik

adj. Coming into existence swiftly, suddenly, brightly, like a meteor.
If Stacey envisaged a **meteoric** rise to fame after her first starring role on Broadway, she was naive.

overbearing
ō vər bâr´ iŋ

adj. Acting in an arrogant, domineering way.
The leading man's **overbearing** manner caused his popularity among the rest of the cast to wane quickly.

precocious
prē kō´ shəs

adj. Showing exceptionally early development of abilities.
The **precocious** child spoke three languages by the time she was seven.

precocity *n.* (pri käs´ ət ē)
Alex's **precocity** in mathematics led to his enrolling in university math classes at the age of sixteen.

proffer
präf´ ər

v. To offer for acceptance or consideration.
The Tai family **proffered** their spare room to an exchange student from China.

n. An offer.
The senior class gladly accepted the **proffer** of the Aldrich Mansion as the site for its graduation party.

remonstrate
rē män´ strāt

v. To say in protest; to raise an objection.
Ms. Newhouse **remonstrated** with Darryl for constantly teasing his classmate Eric.

rift
rift

n. 1. A split or crack.
The **rift** in the rock was too wide for me to jump across.

2. A break in friendly relations.
The **rift** between the brothers became manifest when they refused to talk to each other at the family dinner.

| **solicitous** | *adj.* Showing interest and care; concerned. |
| sə lis′ ə təs | After her appendix was removed, Emily welcomed the **solicitous** calls and visits of her friends. |

| **succinct** | *adj.* Expressed clearly and in few words; concise. |
| sək siŋkt′ | For someone who is usually so voluble, Clark's answers to the principal's questions were remarkably **succinct.** |

| **sylvan** | *adj.* Having to do with trees or wooded areas. |
| sil′ vən | Our drama group chose the **sylvan** setting of Manor Park for our presentation of *A Midsummer Night's Dream.* |

| **trepidation** | *n.* Apprehension; dread. |
| trep ə dā′ shən | The thought that they might be blamed for the accident filled the children with **trepidation.** |

| **untoward** | *adj.* Not favorable; unlucky. |
| un tôrd′ | Despite our fears, nothing **untoward** happened during our climb up Mount Fuji. |

virtuoso	*n.* A person with great skill in some art, especially music.
vɜr chōō ō′ sō	The late pianist Rudolf Serkin was not only a **virtuoso,** but also a performer much loved by audiences for his gentle manner.
	adj. Done with great skill and dash.
	The ten-year-old prodigy gave a **virtuoso** performance of the Brahms concerto.

13A ▶ Understanding Meanings

Read the sentences. If a sentence correctly uses the word in bold, write *C* on the line. If a sentence is incorrect, rewrite it so that the vocabulary word in bold is used correctly.

1. An **overbearing** person is one who is taller or larger than others.

   _____

   _____

2. A **rift** is a falling out between two individuals or groups.

   _____

   _____

3. A **succinct** comment is soothing or comforting.

   _____

   _____

4. To **discomfit** someone is to make that person uncomfortable.

_____

_____

5. **Trepidation** is a feeling of fear of what might happen.

_____

_____

6. To **proffer** something is to sell it to someone.

_____

_____

7. **Blandishments** are threats not meant to be taken seriously.

_____

_____

8. An **untoward** event is one that has unfortunate consequences.

_____

_____

9. A **solicitous** person is one who meddles in other people's affairs.

_____

_____

10. A **meteoric** career is one that has developed quickly and successfully.

_____

_____

11. A **precocious** person is one who is very dearly loved.

_____

_____

blandishment
deprecate
discomfit
meteoric
overbearing
precocious
proffer
remonstrate
rift
solicitous
succinct
sylvan
trepidation
untoward
virtuoso

12. Moonlight would be a dominant element in a **sylvan** painting.

_____

_____

13. A **virtuoso** is one who sings or plays unaccompanied.

_____

_____

14. To **deprecate** something is to make comments that diminish its value.

_____

_____

15. To **remonstrate** with someone is to cooperate with that person on a project.

_____

_____

If the word (or a form of the word) in bold fits in a sentence in the group following it, write the word in the blank space. If the word does not fit, leave the space empty. There may be more than one correct answer.

1. **overbearing**

   (a) Headmaster Winn's _____ ways made him unpopular with his teaching staff.

   (b) My problems were so _____ that I just couldn't handle them.

   (c) We found Pam so _____ that we gave up trying to argue with her.

2. **discomfit**

   (a) I was _____ to discover that the notes for my talk were back at the hotel.

   (b) I expect new shoes to _____ my feet for the first few days that I wear them.

   (c) Cilla urged her hosts not to _____ themselves on her account.

3. **rift**

   (a) A hundred-mile _____ had opened in the ocean floor.

   (b) We each extended a hand, agreeing to heal the _____ between us.

   (c) The knife slipped and made a nasty _____ on the counter.

4. **untoward**

   (a) The ship at first approached us; then it turned around and sailed in an _____ direction.

   (b) Her _____ attitude indicates her lack of interest in going to the party.

   (c) We soon put aside the _____ incidents of our trip and remembered only the good times.

5. **sylvan**

   (a) Biltmore Farm lies at the end of a mile-long _____ drive.

   (b) Great boughs of evergreen contributed to the hall's _____ atmosphere.

   (c) The concrete and skyscrapers gave the city a _____ appearance.

6. **blandishment**

   (a) Clams, oysters, shrimp, and other tasty _____ were served at the supper.

   (b) The gifts were simply _____ intended to overcome her suspicions.

   (c) I refused to yield to his _____ and insisted on keeping my regular job.

7. **deprecate**

    (a) Please don't _____ the contributions of those who helped you.

    (b) The house will _____ in value if you fail to maintain it properly.

    (c) Mr. Snobbish continues to _____ all popular music written after 1950.

8. **proffer**

    (a) He _____ his hand to me in a gesture of friendship.

    (b) I _____ greatly from my speculation in the stock market.

    (c) Tsieng Hu rejected the position of ambassador when it was _____ by the president.

13c ▷ Word Study

The prefix *in-* can mean "not," changing a word to its opposite. However, the letters *in* do not always indicate a prefix. In the spaces provided, write a brief definition of each of the words. Write "yes" if the letters *in* indicate the prefix meaning "not" in each word.

1. incredible   _____   _____

2. infer   _____   _____

3. inexplicable   _____   _____

4. ingenious   _____   _____

5. intangible   _____   _____

6. incontrovertible   _____   _____

7. ingrate   _____   _____

8. induct   _____   _____

9. indolent   _____   _____

10. insuperable   _____   _____

blandishment
deprecate
discomfit
meteoric
overbearing
precocious
proffer
remonstrate
rift
solicitous
succinct
sylvan
trepidation
untoward
virtuoso

Circle the letter of each sentence that suggests the numbered bold vocabulary word. In each group, you may circle more than one letter or none at all.

1. **trepidation**

   (a) Marcia felt her blood run cold when she saw the trap door slowly opening.

   (b) The stage manager had to push me onto the stage on opening night.

   (c) I insisted I could not cross the flimsy rope bridge ahead.

2. **remonstrate**

   (a) Watch how easily the Choppermatic shreds, slices, and dices vegetables.

   (b) "How often must I tell you not to wear my clothes!" said Claire angrily.

   (c) Robyn won the prize for selling the most raffle tickets.

3. **blandishments**

   (a) "The color of this dress suits you perfectly, madam, and it's just your style," said the sales associate.

   (b) We can't watch the movie until we finish our homework.

   (c) Please, I ask you; give me just one more chance!

4. **virtuoso**

   (a) This is a perfectly preserved specimen of a dinosaur's egg.

   (b) During his lifetime, Bach was a famous organist.

   (c) Ruggles led a blameless life and was loved by all who knew him.

5. **succinct**

   (a) When I asked what I could do to help, she said, "Give money."

   (b) The juice squirted out of the orange when I cut it open.

   (c) The spaghetti sauce needs just a little more oregano.

6. **meteoric**

   (a) This rock was formed from the molten lava of a volcano.

   (b) The car was doing at least eighty miles an hour when it passed us.

   (c) Elvis Presley went from unknown singer to international star in less than a year.

7. **precocity**

   (a) Mozart was an accomplished composer by the age of five.

   (b) Most children can talk by the age of two.

   (c) The Delany sisters led active lives until well into their nineties.

8. **solicitous**

   (a) That'll teach you to be more careful in the future.

   (b) I hope you didn't hurt yourself.

   (c) I am voting for Bloggs, the environmental candidate.

9. **deprecate**

    (a) Please don't thank me; I did hardly anything to help.

    (b) You call that a cake! Wait until you taste my almond cream torte!

    (c) This car is worth less than it was last year.

10. **untoward**

    (a) The road ran straight as an arrow for about five miles.

    (b) As we approached the beach, the traffic got heavier.

    (c) The jacket fits perfectly, but the pants are a little tight around the waist.

13E   Passage

Read the passage. Then answer the questions that follow it.

The Gift of Music

The Boston Symphony Orchestra summer concerts, held in the **sylvan** setting of Tanglewood, in western Massachusetts, are world famous. An invitation to perform there as a soloist is a great honor for any musician. But if violinist Midori felt any **trepidation** when she took the stage at Tanglewood for the first time in 1986, she did not show it—even though she was to play Leonard Bernstein's *Serenade*, with the renowned composer himself conducting the orchestra.

Not long after Midori began playing, the E-string on her violin snapped, bringing the music to a complete stop, an experience that could **discomfit** even a seasoned musician. Midori's poise, however, was unshaken. She waited calmly until the concertmaster **proffered** his own violin, and she resumed playing. Then the unthinkable happened. Again the E-string snapped. Again the music was brought to a halt. This time the associate concertmaster came to the rescue. With a second borrowed violin, Midori began where she had left off, playing with unbroken concentration and concluding her performance without any further **untoward** occurrences. When it was over, the music critic of the *New York Times* wrote, "Audience, orchestra, and conductor joined in giving her a cheering, stomping, whistling ovation." Midori was fourteen at the time.

To achieve such acclaim at this early age was extraordinary, but Midori was no ordinary person. Her mother, Setsu Goto, who was a violinist and music teacher in Osaka, Japan, used to take Midori to orchestra rehearsals when she was an infant. Setsu Goto became aware of her daughter's musical **precocity** when she heard two-year-old Midori humming a Bach concerto that the orchestra had been rehearsing two days before. Goto gave her daughter a one-sixteenth-size violin for her third birthday and by the time Midori was eleven she was enrolled at the Juilliard School of Music in New York. She studied under Dorothy DeLay, one of the foremost violin teachers in the country.

blandishment
deprecate
discomfit
meteoric
overbearing
precocious
proffer
remonstrate
rift
solicitous
succinct
sylvan
trepidation
untoward
virtuoso

Midori was lucky, too; she had a wise mother. Unfortunately, many parents of musical prodigies find it difficult to resist the **blandishments** of promoters who would exploit gifted children with promises of lucrative concert and recording contracts. Such parents can become so **overbearing** that they blame the child if a particular orchestra is slow to offer a return engagement, something that can happen for a variety of reasons unrelated to the child's ability. They may also become so **solicitous** of the child that asking their twelve-year-old who has just played in a great symphony hall to do something ordinary like take out the trash seems unthinkable. Setsu Goto strongly **deprecated** such attitudes; she allowed her daughter to have a relatively normal upbringing.

Although Midori is very close to her mother, she is also very independent and strong-willed. When she was fifteen, a **rift** developed between her and Dorothy DeLay that resulted in Midori's quitting Juilliard. Her mother **remonstrated** with her to return, but Midori refused. Later, her **succinct** explanation for this potentially damaging move was: "I felt it was time that I left."

Although she possesses extraordinary natural talent, Midori has always practiced conscientiously. On her eighteenth birthday, she was rewarded with an invitation to play at Carnegie Hall. On that occasion she gave a **virtuoso** performance that established her as one of the world's great violinists. Despite her **meteoric** rise to fame, Midori has not become absorbed only in herself. When she was twenty-one, she set up Midori and Friends, a foundation that brings classical music to children in public schools and hospitals. And even with her busy schedule, she finds the time to give several foundation-related concerts a year.

▶ **Answer each question in the form of a sentence. If a question does not contain a word from the lesson, use one in your answer. Use each word only once.**

1. When did Midori's mother become aware of her daughter's **precocity?**

_____

_____

2. What **untoward** event occurred while Midori was at Tanglewood?

_____

_____

3. When did it become clear that Midori was a **virtuoso?**

_____

_____

4. Why can one infer that Tanglewood summer concerts are held outdoors?

_____

_____

5. Why might Midori's mother have felt **trepidation** for her daughter when she learned she had quit Juilliard?

_____

_____

6. How did Midori show that she was not **discomfited** by the breaking strings?

_____

_____

7. Why did Midori leave Juilliard?

_____

_____

8. What advice might Midori's mother **proffer** to parents of other prodigies?

_____

_____

9. Why is Midori unlikely to succumb to the **blandishments** of promoters?

_____

_____

10. How is it made clear that her mother **deprecated** Midori's decision to quit Juilliard?

_____

_____

11. Why would it be inaccurate to say that Midori spent a lot of time discussing her reasons for quitting Juilliard?

_____

_____

blandishment
deprecate
discomfit
meteoric
overbearing
precocious
proffer
remonstrate
rift
solicitous
succinct
sylvan
trepidation
untoward
virtuoso

FUN & FASCINATING FACTS

- **Discomfit** once meant "to defeat in battle" or "to vanquish." This meaning weakened over time. The word's modern meaning, "to make uneasy," probably came about because of its similarity to *discomfort*, which means "to make less comfortable." One can feel *discomfort*, for example, by wearing tight shoes, without being *discomfited*. However, if one is *discomfited*, for example, by being accused of something, one is bound to be *discomforted* also.

- The Latin for *forest* is *silva*, derived from Silvanus, the Roman god of woods and trees. It forms the root of **sylvan,** "relating to woods and trees" and also to *silviculture*, "the care and cultivation of forest trees."

For more practice and games, go
to **www.WordlyWise3000.com**.

| Word List | Study the definitions of the words. Then do the exercises that follow. |

amass
ə mas´

v. To gather or collect for one's use or profit; to accumulate.
Karen's aptitude for business enabled her to **amass** a small fortune before she was thirty.

articulate
är tik´ yōō lāt´

v. 1. To pronounce distinctly.
Children usually can **articulate** words before they are two years old.

2. To express one's thoughts, feelings, or beliefs in words.
In this essay, I have tried to **articulate** my view of the novel *Jane Eyre.*

adj. (är tik´ yōō lət). Able to speak in clear and effective language.
Winston Churchill's slight speech impediment did not prevent him from being a very **articulate** public speaker.

decimate
des´ ə māt

v. To kill or destroy a large portion of a group.
Cholera swept through the town, **decimating** the population.

dexterous
dek´ stər əs

adj. Skillful in the use of hands or mind.
Her **dexterous** handling of the horse won her a blue ribbon.

dexterity *n.* (dek stêr´ ə tē)
Repairing the fishing nets would require a **dexterity** that Franklin lacked.

garb
gärb

n. A style of clothing; costume.
Queen Victoria's black **garb** and solemn demeanor were constant reminders of her widow's state.

v. To clothe or dress.
The old photos showed nomadic people of Turkistan **garbed** in intricately patterned robes.

gregarious
grə ger´ ē əs

adj. Enjoying the company of others; sociable.
A **gregarious** nature is a boon for anyone seeking a political career.

inherent
in hir´ ənt

adj. Existing as a natural part of something.
Believing her shyness is **inherent,** Roseanne does nothing to try to overcome it.

maternal
mə tʉr´ nəl

adj. 1. Motherly.
Ranji's **maternal** feelings were aroused when she saw a child standing alone weeping at the bus stop.

2. Related to or inherited through one's mother.
My **maternal** grandparents had two children, my mother and my uncle Bill.

nurture	*v.* To care for and give sustenance to.
nʉr´ chər	Parents **nurture** their children physically, mentally, and psychologically.
	n. The process of raising one's young.
	Both male and female emperor penguins provide **nurture** for their young chicks.

obtrusive	*adj.* 1. Tending to push oneself forward in an unwelcome manner.
äb trōō´ siv	The reporters at the house were so **obtrusive** that Belle slammed the door in their faces.
	2. Noticeable in an undesirable way.
	Dressed in jeans, we felt **obtrusive** as we entered the small, elegant restaurant.

parody	*v.* To imitate the style of someone or something in order to make fun of it.
per´ ə dē	The film *Bad Guys in Black Hats* **parodies** western movies of the 1930s.
	n. An imitation that exaggerates for comic effect.
	His **parody** of Lincoln's "Gettysburg Address" that began, "I believe it was about eighty years ago . . ." showed poor taste.

pugnacious	*adj.* Aggressive; eager to fight or quarrel.
pug nā´ shəs	The **pugnacious** basketball player challenged the referee with insulting words.
	pugnacity *n.* (pug nas´ ə tē)
	He showed his **pugnacity** by clenching his fists.

| **reprehensible** | *adj.* Deserving blame or rebuke. |
| rep´ rē hen´ sə bəl | Denying sustenance to those in need is **reprehensible.** |

| **tractable** | *adj.* Easily managed or controlled. |
| trak´ tə bəl | The stable manager gave Jennifer a **tractable** horse when she first began riding. |

| **zany** | *adj.* Comical because of strangeness; clownish. |
| zā´ nē | The **zany** illustrations make the book very popular. |

14A ▶ Understanding Meanings

Read the sentences. If a sentence correctly uses the word in bold, write *C* on the line. If a sentence is incorrect, rewrite it so that the vocabulary word in bold is used correctly.

1. A **gregarious** person is one given to sudden mood changes.

   _____

   _____

2. **Maternal** affection is like that shown by a mother to her children.

   _____

   _____

3. A **zany** outfit is noticeable for its somber colors.

_____

_____

4. To **amass** wealth is to acquire it in large amounts.

_____

_____

5. **Dexterity** is a state of indifference to one's surroundings.

_____

_____

6. A **tractable** creature is one that is easily guided.

_____

_____

7. To **articulate** ideas is to express them clearly.

_____

_____

8. To **parody** something is to evade it.

_____

_____

9. A **pugnacious** person is one who goes looking for a fight.

_____

_____

10. To **decimate** an army is to divide it into ten equal units.

_____

_____

11. To act in an **obtrusive** manner is to be compulsive in behavior.

_____

_____

12. To **garb** someone is to pull at that person's clothes.

_____

_____

13. A **reprehensible** statement is one that is difficult to understand.

_____

_____

14. To **nurture** a project is to watch over it to see that it grows and develops.

_____

_____

15. An **inherent** virtue is one that is barely noticeable.

_____

_____

If the word (or a form of the word) in bold fits in a sentence in the group following it, write the word in the blank space. If the word does not fit, leave the space empty. There may be more than one correct answer.

1. **obtrusive**

   (a) The noise of the children's voices was so _____ that I was unable to read my book.

   (b) Our neighbors are less _____ now that we have a lock on the gate.

   (c) The answer was so _____ that I didn't even have to think about it.

2. **reprehensible**

   (a) Such _____ behavior will not go unpunished.

   (b) Cutting pages from library books is _____ .

   (c) Her handwriting is so bad that it is barely _____ .

3. **decimate**

   (a) If you _____ $^3/_4$, you get 0.75.

   (b) The only way to _____ weeds is to pull them up by the roots.

   (c) The unusual virus _____ the population of the city.

4. **amass**

   (a) See how the birds _____ in the trees before flying south.

   (b) She will _____ all the necessary information before writing the report.

   (c) The reporter _____ a large amount of information, but much of it he wouldn't use in the article.

5. **garb**

   (a) Deena's customary _____ was a T-shirt and jeans.

   (b) Robin Hood's merry men were _____ in forest green.

   (c) She took a black silk _____ from the rack and held it against herself.

amass
articulate
decimate
dexterous
garb
gregarious
inherent
maternal
nurture
obtrusive
parody
pugnacious
reprehensible
tractable
zany

6. **articulate**

(a) One expects members of a college debating team to be _____ .

(b) The parrot could _____ a few French words.

(c) At the conference, the scientist _____ her views on climate change.

7. **zany**

(a) The book describes in detail the _____ world of the Marx Brothers.

(b) The _____ movies featuring the Three Stooges made millions laugh.

(c) Whose _____ idea was it to use an air horn to scare off the birds?

8. **nurture**

(a) Good teachers try to _____ each student's abilities.

(b) These are matters of a personal _____ that I discuss only with my doctor.

(c) Classes dealing with the proper _____ of infants are held every Monday.

14c Word Study

Each group of words contains two words that are either synonyms or antonyms. Circle them. Then circle *S* if they are synonyms or *A* if they are antonyms.

1. reprehensible	useful	gregarious	blameless	S	A
2. acquire	amass	traverse	nurture	S	A
3. fashion	solace	skill	vogue	S	A
4. gregarious	inherent	solitary	practicable	S	A
5. adversity	faculty	dexterity	misfortune	S	A
6. untoward	advanced	precocious	similar	S	A
7. pernicious	harmless	pensive	helpless	S	A
8. pariah	prodigy	proffer	offer	S	A
9. quandary	trepidation	blandishment	confidence	S	A
10. discomfit	embarrass	deprecate	defray	S	A

Circle the letter of each sentence that suggests the numbered bold vocabulary word. In each group, you may circle more than one letter or none at all.

1. **dexterous**

   (a) Josie usually solves the *Times* crossword puzzle in fifteen minutes.

   (b) Charlie could juggle five balls at the same time.

   (c) I can read a car license plate from fifty feet.

2. **nurture**

   (a) The house was strong enough to withstand hurricanes with 120 mph winds.

   (b) Elizabeth Taylor starred in *National Velvet* at the age of twelve.

   (c) Macaws and cockatoos are noted for their longevity and their ability to mimic speech.

3. **pugnacity**

   (a) "What do you think you are doing?" he interrupted boldly.

   (b) "Do you need help?" he asked kindly.

   (c) "I couldn't care less," he drawled apathetically.

4. **decimate**

   (a) In the 1980s, deaths from AIDS were especially numerous in San Francisco and New York City.

   (b) During the Allied invasion of Normandy, the first wave of troops took extremely heavy casualties.

   (c) I cut the pizza into ten slices and gave one to each child.

5. **gregarious**

   (a) The campers in the next tent invited us to join in their sing-along.

   (b) When Sammy got the measles, his sister knew she would get the disease, too.

   (c) The Robinsons seem to know just about everyone in town.

6. **articulate**

   (a) The deadline to register for second semester is next Monday.

   (b) "Now . . . do . . . you . . . understand?" he asked, stressing every syllable.

   (c) The Surgeon General's views on smoking have been expressed many times.

7. **inherent**

   (a) When my grandmother died, she left me her beautiful antique jewelry.

   (b) It is foolish to complain that lemons are sour.

   (c) People often say my smile is the same as my mother's.

amass
articulate
decimate
dexterous
garb
gregarious
inherent
maternal
nurture
obtrusive
parody
pugnacious
reprehensible
tractable
zany

8. **tractable**

(a) The farmer hoped for a good harvest so he could use some of the profits to purchase modern machinery.

(b) Simon can do a very good sketch in less than a minute.

(c) Once children get past the "terrible twos," they are more agreeable.

9. **parody**

(a) What a wonderful view of the valley you have from this window!

(b) The audience laughed hilariously at the Miami Players' "Five-Minute Macbeth."

(c) The revised sonnet begins, "Shall I compare thee to a ripe tomato?"

10. **maternal**

(a) My mother comes from a large family, so I have many aunts and uncles.

(b) Holding the baby stirred Alice's memories of her own children, now grown up.

(c) Strong leadership marked the reign of Elizabeth I.

14E Passage

Read the passage. Then answer the questions that follow it.

Close Relatives

The image of the chimpanzee some of us may have is that of a creature who can make us laugh at what seems a comical **parody** of human behavior. We may even have seen chimps on television or in the circus, often in human **garb,** performing as they have been trained, amusing the audience with their **zany** antics.

Chimpanzees are not **inherently** comical. In fact, they are strong, highly intelligent, lively primates, members of the order of mammals that includes humans as well as apes. They are more like human beings—in their genes, their body and brain structure, and the way their organs work—than are any other living beings. Research has shown that our human gene code differs from that of chimpanzees by less than two percent: more than ninety-eight percent of our genes are the same. Chimpanzees are capable of reasoning, of abstraction, and of other intellectual processes that we used to think only humans possessed. Chimpanzees have language capability, even though they cannot **articulate** human speech. A young chimp is able to make at least thirty-two different sounds, and its face can express a wide range of emotions. **Tractable** animals, they have learned to communicate using American Sign Language or computer keyboards.

Chimpanzees also have emotions similar to ours. They, too, experience happiness and sadness, fear and anxiety. They have a sense of humor, and develop close friendships with other individuals; they become distressed if separated from a companion and grieve if one dies.

Found mostly in the tropical forests and grasslands of Africa, they are **gregarious** creatures, and live in highly organized communities of from fifteen to eighty adult males, females, infants, and partly grown young. The average size of a chimpanzee is about 4 ½ feet tall with a weight of about 120 pounds. They have long arms and short legs, large ears, abundant brown or black hair, and often a white area around the mouth. Unlike monkeys, they have no tail. They live both high up in the trees and on the ground. In the trees, where most feeding takes place, they swing from branch to branch; when on the ground, although they are able to walk erect, they usually walk on all fours, using the knuckles of their hands. Young chimpanzees are playful and affectionate; adults are extremely powerful—much more powerful than people— and can be **pugnacious** if taken from their natural habitat into captivity.

Males and females cooperate in providing and sharing food. Although their diet is mainly vegetarian, chimpanzees also eat meat. Males form hunting parties to stalk smaller mammals such as monkeys, young baboons, and bush pigs. Because the females have strong **maternal** instincts and **nurture** their young for as long as four years, their ability to join in the hunt is restricted. Instead, they gather food, collecting fruit, plants, insects, and birds' eggs. Being especially **dexterous,** chimpanzees are able to make the tools they need. Females, for example, strip long twigs and poke them through holes in termite hills. When they carefully withdraw the stick, termites are clinging to it; these can then be removed and eaten.

Much of what we know about chimpanzees comes from the work of the English anthropologist Jane Goodall. She has been studying chimpanzees' behavior in the central African country of Tanzania since 1960. By living among them as **unobtrusively** as possible, she has been able to observe and record their activities. Over several decades she has **amassed** a vast amount of information while campaigning in their behalf. In 1968 she persuaded the Tanzanian government to establish Gombe National Park as a chimpanzee sanctuary and research center.

In recent years, Africa's chimpanzee population has been **decimated.** Their numbers have been reduced by such **reprehensible** practices as illegal hunting and the destruction of the tropical rain forest by logging or farming. They are also subject to capture for use in zoos and research laboratories. They are now an endangered species.

amass
articulate
decimate
dexterous
garb
gregarious
inherent
maternal
nurture
obtrusive
parody
pugnacious
reprehensible
tractable
zany

▶ **Answer each question in the form of a sentence. If a question does not contain a word from the lesson, use one in your answer. Use each word only once.**

1. Why would chimpanzees be clad in human **garb?**

_____

_____

2. How can a chimpanzee's behavior change if it is captured and taken from its habitat?

_____

_____

3. In what ways are humans and chimpanzees **inherently** the same?

_____

_____

4. In your opinion, is destroying chimpanzee habitats for logging or farming **reprehensible?**

_____

_____

5. How do female chimpanzees demonstrate **maternal** instincts?

_____

_____

6. Why do chimpanzees in the wild live in groups?

_____

_____

7. According to the passage, what contribution has Jane Goodall made?

_____

_____

8. What significant difference is there between chimpanzees and humans?

_____

_____

9. How has their dexterity and the fact that they are **tractable** animals allowed chimpanzees to communicate with humans?

_____

_____

10. Why is the chimpanzee in danger of extinction if present trends continue?

_____

_____

11. How was Goodall able to gather so much information?

_____

_____

12. Would you find the behavior of performing chimpanzees **zany?**

_____

_____

The Latin *decimus* means "one tenth" and forms the root of *decimal* (a number written using the base of ten) and *decimeter* (a unit of length equal to one tenth of a meter). The verb **decimate** has the same root and offers a glimpse into Roman history. A legion that mutinied or showed cowardice in the face of the enemy could be **decimated** as a punishment. One person out of ten, chosen by lot, would be executed. The word retains its original meaning but has become less precise. It is possible to speak of an army being *decimated* in battle even though it lost more than (though probably not less than) one tenth of its strength.

In Lesson 8, you learned that *adroit* means "skillful" and comes from the French *a droit*, which means "to the right." The idea that the right side is superior to the left goes back to Roman times, when priests regarded signs from the left as foretelling misfortune. **Dexterous** has a similar meaning to adroit and comes from the Latin *dexter*, "on the right side." In medieval times, heraldic shields were divided between left and right. The side on the bearer's right was the dexter side; that on the bearer's left was the sinister side, from the Latin *sinister*, "on the left."

The Latin *greg* means "herd" or "flock" and forms the root of *congregate*, "to come together as a group," and *segregate*, "to separate from others." The adjective **gregarious** is formed from the same root. A *gregarious* person likes to be with a group, enjoying the company of others.

amass

articulate

decimate

dexterous

garb

gregarious

inherent

maternal

nurture

obtrusive

parody

pugnacious

reprehensible

tractable

zany

| Word List | Study the definitions of the words. Then do the exercises that follow. |

accentuate
ak sen´ choo āt´

v. To emphasize or stress.
The tall crown of that hat **accentuates** Becky's height.

aficionado
ə fish ē ə näd´ ō

n. An enthusiastic follower; a supporter or fan.
"Star Trek" **aficionados** eagerly awaited the next episode.

antecedent
an tə sēd´ nt

n. A thing or event that precedes another.
Robert Fulton's 1801 submersible craft was the **antecedent** of the modern submarine.

adj. Going before; preceding.
Many years of research were **antecedent** to this drug's being sold without a prescription.

centrifugal
sen trif´ yə gəl

adj. Moving or tending away from the center.
If the string snaps on the toy that you are swinging, **centrifugal** force will send it flying away from you.

convoluted
kän´ və loot əd

adj. 1. Having numerous coils or folds.
That flexible wire can be twisted into **convoluted** shapes.

2. Complicated; intricate.
The jurors had difficulty following the **convoluted** explanation of the witness.

decapitate
dē kap´ ə tāt´

v. To kill by cutting off the head.
During the French Revolution those marked for execution were **decapitated** by the guillotine.

disingenuous
dis n jen´ yə wəs

adj. Not straightforward; insincere.
"I would be **disingenuous** if I told you there were only a few things wrong with your teeth," the dentist said.

indubitable
in doo´ bi tə bəl

adj. Too evident to be doubted; unquestionable.
Your signature on this paper is **indubitable** proof that you are a co-owner of the cabin.

jaded
jād´ əd

adj. Dulled or wearied by excess or overindulgence.
Jaded fans of special effects in movies seem to need ever more spectacular sights in order to be thrilled.

masochistic
mas ə kis´ tik

adj. Deriving pleasure from being mistreated mentally or physically.
The Boston bathers who enter the frigid waters annually on New Year's Day denied they were **masochistic,** but claimed instead simply to enjoy the experience.

masochist *n.*
"Only a **masochist** would choose to live in the wilderness for a week with no equipment," asserted Charlene.

momentum mō men′ təm	*n.* Force or speed of movement; force or energy that keeps something moving. Senator Clay's presidential campaign lost **momentum** because she was late entering the New Hampshire primary.
obsolescent äb sə les′ ənt	*adj.* Going out of use; becoming obsolete. Typewriters are **obsolescent** now that personal computers are so common.
potential pō ten′ shəl	*adj.* Having possibility or capability. Light and heat from the sun are **potential** sources of energy that could be a boon to humanity. *n.* The capacity for growth or development. The abandoned factory building has considerable **potential** as a site for the proposed recycling center.
viscera vis′ ər ə	*n. pl.* The internal organs of the body. The **viscera** include the liver, pancreas, and intestines. **visceral** *adj.* Felt strongly, as if in the viscera. When she realized the plant in her hand was covered with slugs, her **visceral** response was to scream.
volition vō lish′ ən	*n.* An act of consciously choosing or deciding. Dan, of his own **volition,** helped us clean up the table and wash the dinner dishes.

15A ▷ Understanding Meanings

accentuate
aficionado
antecedent
centrifugal
convoluted
decapitate
disingenuous
indubitable
jaded
masochistic
momentum
obsolescent
potential
viscera
volition

Read the sentences. If a sentence correctly uses the word in bold, write C on the line. If a sentence is incorrect, rewrite it so that the vocabulary word in bold is used correctly.

1. **Indubitable** facts are those that are certain.

   _____

   _____

2. A **disingenuous** statement is one that is extremely insulting.

   _____

   _____

3. A **masochist** is a person who chews his or her food thoroughly.

   _____

   _____

4. A **jaded** appetite is one that cannot be satisfied.

   _____

   _____

5. **Centrifugal** tendencies are those causing movement away from the center.

_____

_____

6. **Volition** is the ability to fly.

_____

_____

7. An **aficionado** is someone who possesses extraordinary skill.

_____

_____

8. A **convoluted** explanation is one that is difficult to follow.

_____

_____

9. An **obsolescent** machine is one that needs to be repaired.

_____

_____

10. **Antecedent** rights are those that existed before ones that came later.

_____

_____

11. **Viscera** are sense organs.

_____

_____

12. A **potential** profit is one that may develop into an actual one.

_____

_____

13. To **accentuate** a word is to put an accent mark in the right place.

_____

_____

14. To **decapitate** someone is to behead him or her.

_____

_____

15. **Momentum** is a single instant of time.

_____

_____

If the word (or a form of the word) in bold fits in a sentence in the group following it, write the word in the blank space. If the word does not fit, leave the space empty. There may be more than one correct answer.

1. **jaded**
   (a) Even though she had won the top tennis tournaments several times, she wasn't _____ from all the attention and money she received.
   (b) We felt so _____ after our climb that we had to sit down and rest.
   (c) I was so _____ by the book that I couldn't read beyond the first chapter.

2. **disingenuous**
   (a) This double-ratcheted widget is a most _____ little device.
   (b) She was being _____ when she let you believe she enjoyed your company.
   (c) My cramped quarters revealed just how _____ the reservations agent had been in describing the room as luxury class.

3. **accentuate**
   (a) The senator's speeches _____ the plight of the small family farm.
   (b) Depending on which word you _____ , you change the meaning slightly.
   (c) We'll _____ the positive and play down the negative aspects of the situation.

4. **potential**
   (a) The new shortstop for the Blue Jays has the _____ to be a great hitter.
   (b) Here is a list of _____ buyers for the property.
   (c) Six thousand dollars is a _____ sum of money.

5. **masochistic**
   (a) Pleasure and pain are mingled in a _____ personality.
   (b) The _____ counselor listened carefully to Sean's problem and then gave several practical suggestions.
   (c) Gerald gave my hand a _____ shake and then headed for the door.

6. **convoluted**
   (a) Kimberly is trying to simplify her _____ writing style.
   (b) The _____ shape in the painting resembled a ram's horn.
   (c) After the car accident, Harry had a two-week _____ period at home.

accentuate
aficionado
antecedent
centrifugal
convoluted
decapitate
disingenuous
indubitable
jaded
masochistic
momentum
obsolescent
potential
viscera
volition

7. **centrifugal**

    (a) Raising the necessary funds is _____ to the success of the youth concerts.

    (b) A boulder perched on the edge of a cliff possesses _____ energy.

    (c) The moon orbits Earth because gravity and _____ force are in balance.

8. **obsolescent**

    (a) As particular jobs become _____ , workers need to retrain for others.

    (b) MP3s are making other forms of recorded music _____ .

    (c) "Prithee" and "methinks" are _____ expressions.

15c Word Study

Complete the analogies by selecting the pair of words whose relationship most resembles the relationship of the pair in capital letters. Circle the letter in front of the pair you choose.

1. ACCENTUATE : SPEECH ::
   (a) divulge : secret   (c) nurture : child
   (b) underline : writing   (d) articulate : discuss

2. SUCCINCT : BREVITY ::
   (a) restless : repose   (c) indolent : alacrity
   (b) magnanimous : cruelty   (d) stilted : awkwardness

3. SOLACE : SORROW ::
   (a) paucity : abundance   (c) sustenance : hunger
   (b) momentum : motion   (d) volition : choice

4. DISTRESSING : HARROWING ::
   (a) costly : gratis   (c) friendly : amorous
   (b) articulated : convoluted (d) actual : potential

5. VISCERAL : ORGANS ::
   (a) mental : brain   (c) solicitous : solace
   (b) disingenuous : ingenuity (d) sylvan : forest

6. CLOWN : ZANY ::
   (a) remark : facetious   (c) rift : rudimentary
   (b) despot : military   (d) partner: amorous

7. INDUBITABLE : DOUBT ::
   (a) definitive : definition   (c) pernicious : harm
   (b) inexplicable : reason   (d) afraid : trepidation

8. ARTICULATE : CLEAR ::
   (a) overbearing : manner
   (b) gregarious : talkative
   (c) ubiquitous : space
   (d) blurry : vision

9. DEXTERITY : HAND ::
   (a) agility : body
   (b) alacrity : speed
   (c) fallacy : idea
   (d) centrifugal : center

10. DISINGENUOUS : DECEIVE ::
    (a) amusing : entertain
    (b) zany : laugh
    (c) amorous : offend
    (d) voluble : speak

15D Images of Words

Circle the letter of each sentence that suggests the numbered bold vocabulary word. In each group, you may circle more than one letter or none at all.

1. **indubitable**
   (a) The capital of Montana is Helena.
   (b) The best place to live in Florida is Gainesville.
   (c) There are seven letters in the word "Arizona."

2. **decapitate**
   (a) e. e. cummings wrote all his poems in lowercase letters.
   (b) Surgeons removed the patient's leg at the knee.
   (c) The coach asked the ballplayer to take off his hat.

3. **visceral**
   (a) Rob had a feeling in the pit of his stomach that there was danger ahead.
   (b) The liver, pancreas, and intestines are part of the digestive tract.
   (c) Mr. Vasquez does not allow his heart to rule his head.

4. **aficionado**
   (a) Rosa has never missed a New York Knicks home game in ten years.
   (b) Theresa and her cousin were very fond of each other.
   (c) Jules followed the chess tournament with keen interest.

5. **convoluted**
   (a) The surface of the brain is deeply folded in on itself.
   (b) The square root of forty-nine is seven.
   (c) The inner workings of a computer remain a mystery to me.

6. **volition**
   (a) The boulder became dislodged and rolled down the hill.
   (b) Roger's father didn't force him to enlist in the Navy.
   (c) Criminals should be held responsible for their actions.

accentuate
aficionado
antecedent
centrifugal
convoluted
decapitate
disingenuous
indubitable
jaded
masochistic
momentum
obsolescent
potential
viscera
volition

7. **potential**

   (a) With this discount, anyone driving an older car might be interested in buying a new one.

   (b) Supervisors can identify workers likely to move into positions of management.

   (c) The business had been poorly run, but I think it could be made to turn a profit.

8. **masochistic**

   (a) For years, Cynthia had lived in pain without complaining.

   (b) Jay was always putting things down and forgetting where he'd left them.

   (c) The guests sat down at a table loaded with delicacies of all kinds.

9. **antecedent**

   (a) My first car, bought many years ago, was very noisy compared to the model I own today.

   (b) The leaden skies should have warned us that a heavy snow was coming.

   (c) The principal said, "If I let you do it, then everyone will want to do it."

10. **momentum**

    (a) The speed of a falling object increases with each passing moment.

    (b) There are sixty seconds in a minute, and sixty minutes in an hour.

    (c) The new math program began in one school, and soon many schools throughout the state were using it.

15E Passage

Read the passage. Then answer the questions that follow it.

The Great American Scream Machine

When it comes to roller coasters, there are two kinds of people—those who cannot wait to get on one and those who wouldn't ride one if they were paid to do so. Ever since the first roller coaster opened for business at Coney Island in 1884, millions of people have lined up for a ride. But the **antecedent** of the roller coaster goes back much further in time. Its origin has been traced to Catherine the Great, who ruled Russia from 1762 to 1796. She had snow packed to form a long slide with a few bumps at the bottom; she then would gather members of her court to ride down with her on a sled. Of course, the ride she offered was much calmer than the three minutes of bone-shaking, terror-filled, stomach-churning fun that roller coaster riders enjoy today.

That thrill-seekers ride these machines of their own **volition,** and pay for the privilege, astonishes those who regard such behavior as clear evidence of a **masochistic** personality. One such enthusiast, a mild-mannered computer operator, holds the record for riding the famous roller coaster of Kings Island, outside Cincinnati, known as the Beast: five thousand times and counting!

The Beast begins with a long, slow, ratchety climb. This serves two purposes. First, it gives the strapped-in occupants plenty of time to anticipate the moment when the cars go over the top. Second, by elevating the cars, which when occupied weigh fifteen tons, to a height of nearly two hundred feet, it stores up enormous **potential** energy. This energy provides the **momentum** for the rest of the ride. Even the most **jaded** riders experience a feeling of mingled terror and excitement as the cars make their first plunge downward. It is a sensation that has been compared to driving over a hundred-foot cliff. Straight ahead is a tunnel that seems to have no overhead clearance. The riders duck as they hurtle toward it at 65 miles per hour. But they clear it with feet to spare. The Beast has never **decapitated** anyone.

The force of gravity felt by a person with both feet on the ground is measured at 1 g.* When a person rides the Beast, this is reduced to 0.2 g on the drops and then is instantly increased to 3.5 g on the upswings. This causes the weight of a 150-pound rider to go from thirty pounds to four-hundred pounds in a split second. Making sharp turns at high speed adds to the Beast's excitement. **Centrifugal** force threatens to hurl the cars off into space. But since the track is banked at an angle of sixty-five degrees, all the pull is downward, keeping the riders glued firmly to their seats but doing unpleasant things to their **viscera.**

The Beast has wooden tracks, a type now considered **obsolescent** in the industry. These tracks give the cars a satisfying clackety-clack sound as they go over the joints, while the riders are maintained in a more or less upright position. Modern roller coaster tracks are made of steel, and the relative merits of the two types is a subject endlessly debated by **aficionados.** Some fans argue that steel is preferable for the tracks because of its greater flexibility. It can be twisted into loops, corkscrews, and other **convoluted** shapes the designers dream up in their pursuit of bigger thrills. But because the steel tracks are coated with neoprene, a synthetic form of rubber, the cars run smoothly and silently. This absence of sound is a major drawback, according to those who champion wooden tracks.

The names given to roller coasters—the Beast, the Cyclone, King Cobra, Shock Wave—suggest danger, an aspect of roller coastering that promoters understandably like to **accentuate.** In doing so, however, they are being somewhat **disingenuous.** Despite their names, roller coasters are safer than children's merry-go-rounds. This is an **indubitable** fact well hidden by the industry but borne out by the relative cost of insuring both rides against accidents. People can act foolishly on merry-go-rounds, jumping on or off when they are in motion, for example. On roller coasters, the riders are restrained. Opportunities for reckless behavior are almost nonexistent. The odds against having a fatal accident while riding a roller coaster are about one-hundred million to one. But after all, the whole point of riding the roller coaster is to scare yourself to death—while knowing all the time that you are really perfectly safe.

accentuate

aficionado

antecedent

centrifugal

convoluted

decapitate

disingenuous

indubitable

jaded

masochistic

momentum

obsolescent

potential

viscera

volition

* *g* represents the gravitational field of Earth. The force of gravity acting on a person standing on Earth is felt as his weight. 2 g would mean the person would suddenly feel twice as heavy as he normally does.

▶ **Answer each question in the form of a sentence. If a question does not contain a word from the lesson, use one in your answer. Use each word only once.**

1. Do you consider it **masochistic** to ride on a roller coaster? Explain your answer.

   _____

   _____

2. In what sense is riding a roller coaster literally a **visceral** experience?

   _____

   _____

3. Is **jaded** a good word to describe a roller coaster **aficionado?**

   _____

   _____

4. Why do riders of the Beast duck as they hurtle toward the tunnel?

   _____

   _____

5. What increases as the roller coaster plunges earthward?

   _____

   _____

6. What would happen to the cars on a bend if the track were not banked?

   _____

   _____

7. What happened when steel roller coaster tracks were introduced?

   _____

   _____

8. How did steel tracks change the roller coaster ride?

   _____

   _____

9. Why don't promoters **accentuate** the safety of roller coasters?

   _____

   _____

10. Explain the origin of the roller coaster.

   _____

   _____

11. What is one **indubitable** fact you learned from this passage?

   _____

   _____

12. Why is it **disingenuous** to insist that a roller coaster is an amusement park's most dangerous ride?

_____

_____

13. How do you know the roller coaster is a popular ride?

_____

_____

FUN & FASCINATING FACTS

- **Antecedent** has a grammatical meaning in addition to those given in the word list. It is the term for a word, phrase, or clause to which a pronoun refers. In the sentence, "Sybil has so much energy that she never seems to get tired," the proper noun *Sybil* is the antecedent of the pronoun *she*. In the sentence, "Tom and his brothers will come back when they are ready," the phrase *Tom and his brothers* is the antecedent of the pronoun *they*.

- **Centrifugal** is formed from the Latin *centrum*, "center," and *fugere*, "to flee." *Centrifugal* force tends to make an object in motion fly away from the center of motion. *Centripetal* force, from the Latin *centrum* and *petere*, "to go toward," acts in the oppo-site direction. Were it not for gravity's *centripetal* force, which holds the moon in Earth's orbit, a satellite would go flying off into outer space because of the *centrifugal* force of its forward motion.

- *Sadism* means "deriving pleasure from inflicting pain on others." The term comes from the scandalous Marquis de Sade (1740–1814), a French nobleman who wrote novels whose characters took pleasure from inflicting pain on others. **Masochism,** on the other hand, means "deriving pleasure from being physically or emotionally abused oneself." The term comes from the Austrian novelist Leopold von Sacher-Masoch (1836–1895), who describes the condition in one of his novels.

accentuate

aficionado

antecedent

centrifugal

convoluted

decapitate

disingenuous

indubitable

jaded

masochistic

momentum

obsolescent

potential

viscera

volition

For more practice and games, go to **www.WordlyWise3000.com**.

Word List	Study the definitions of the words. Then do the exercises that follow.

belated
bə lāt´ əd

adj. Done too late; having been delayed beyond the usual time.
Kofi's **belated** birthday card arrived one month after my birthday.

caliber
kal´ i bər

n. 1. Degree of importance or excellence.
The college faculty is of the highest **caliber** and includes several Nobel Prize winners.

2. The diameter of a bullet or inside of a gun barrel.
A .45-**caliber** bullet is 45/100 of an inch in diameter.

chagrin
shə grin´

n. A feeling of embarrassment or annoyance caused by having failed or being disappointed.
To my **chagrin** I twisted my ankle as I attempted to make a jump while skating.

v. To cause to feel unease.
I was quite **chagrined** by my date's failure to meet me as planned.

contravene
kän trə vēn´

v. To act against or be counter to.
The personnel director reprimanded the employee for **contravening** the company policy of no smoking.

default
dē fôlt´

n. 1. Failure to do what is required by duty or law.
When her opponent failed to appear, Nora won the chess game by **default.**

2. An automatic selection made according to a computer program when the user does not make a choice.
The **default** was to close the file before quitting.

v. To fail to pay what or when one should.
The bank will repossess the car if you **default** on your car loan.

doldrums
dōl´ drəmz

n. pl. A condition of feeling sad, bored, or sluggish.
I was in the **doldrums** about my career until I received an exciting job offer in Costa Rica.

emblazon
em blā´ zən

v. To inscribe or decorate conspicuously.
The team sponsor's name was **emblazoned** across the backs of the players' jerseys.

eminent
em´ ə nənt

adj. Standing above others in worth, rank, or fame.
In the late 1700s, **eminent** inventor and engineer Eli Whitney constructed the cotton gin, an invention that changed the way cotton crops were harvested.

eminence *n.*
Octavio Paz's **eminence** as a writer of Latin American literature has led to his books' inclusion on many college reading lists.

expend
ek spend´

v. To use up; consume.
Sedentary office workers do not **expend** much physical energy on the job.

expire ek spīr´	*v.* 1. To come to an end. Unless I renew it, my fishing license will **expire** next month. 2. To die. The patient **expired** before he could be rushed to the hospital.
exponent ek spō´ nənt	*n.* A person who explains, interprets, or works to make something popular. Alvin Ailey, who founded the American Dance Theatre in 1958, was an **exponent** of a kind of modern dance that often incorporated African elements.
novice näv´ is	*n.* A person new at something; a beginner. Although I am only a **novice** at downhill skiing, I find the sport exhilarating.
spry sprī	*adj.* Moving with quickness and ease; lively. The lethargic cat lay curled up in front of the fire while the **spry** kitten leaped from the chair, to the table, to the top of the refrigerator.
tenuous ten´ yōō əs	*adj.* 1. Lacking substance, flimsy. His argument that demolishing the historic building would enhance the appearance of the street is indeed **tenuous.** 2. Not thick; slender. The **tenuous** length of rope was rejected by the hikers in favor of a stronger piece. 3. Lacking density; thin. At an altitude of 29,000 feet, the air is **tenuous,** making it necessary for mountain climbers to rely on supplementary oxygen.
truism trōō´ iz əm	*n.* A truth that is so well known that it is almost unnecessary to say it. "You only live once" is a **truism.**

16A ▷ Understanding Meanings

Read the sentences. If a sentence correctly uses the word in bold, write *C* on the line. If a sentence is incorrect, rewrite it so that the vocabulary word in bold is used correctly.

1. A **tenuous** connection is one that is easily broken.

_____

_____

2. A **truism** is a false statement that appears to be true.

_____

_____

3. To **default** on something is to be falsely blamed for it.

_____

_____

4. To **contravene** a rule is to be governed by it.

_____

_____

5. A **belated** welcome is one that is given too long after a person arrives.

_____

_____

6. To **expend** precious resources is to deplete them.

_____

_____

7. To **expire** is to draw one's last breath.

_____

_____

8. An **eminent** poet is one who has recently died.

_____

_____

9. To **emblazon** a uniform is to add attention-getting details to it.

_____

_____

10. An **exponent** of universal health care is someone who favors it.

_____

_____

11. To be in the **doldrums** is to be in a state of apathetic inactivity.

_____

_____

12. A **spry** person is one who meddles in the affairs of others.

_____

_____

13. A **novice** is someone who is inexperienced.

_____

_____

14. **Chagrin** is fear of the unknown.

_____

_____

15. The **caliber** of a gun measures the inside diameter of the barrel.

_____

_____

16B ▶ Using Words

If the word (or a form of the word) in bold fits in a sentence in the group following it, write the word in the blank space. If the word does not fit, leave the space empty. There may be more than one correct answer.

1. **default**

   (a) I _____ her for not making a greater effort in her course work.

   (b) After _____ on so many financial obligations, he had to declare bankruptcy.

   (c) When Nuñez walked off the court in a huff, I won the match by _____ .

2. **exponent**

   (a) The president says he is an _____ of free trade.

   (b) The writer of Mother Goose, a collection of verse for children, was an _____ of rhymed poetry.

   (c) I defeated my _____ in the chess tournament in fifteen moves.

3. **belated**

   (a) I offer you _____ congratulations on last month's promotion to chair of the department.

   (b) The _____ patrons had to stand since all the seats were taken.

   (c) We were _____ to hear that Trixie won "Best Cat in Show."

4. **doldrums**

   (a) The state has big plans to rescue its tourist industry from the _____ .

   (b) I told him to snap out of the _____ and go out and do something he enjoys.

   (c) Few businesses survived the economic _____ of the 1930s.

belated

caliber

chagrin

contravene

default

doldrums

emblazon

eminent

expend

expire

exponent

novice

spry

tenuous

truism

5. **eminent**

   (a) Her _____ reputation as a philanthropist made her a beloved figure in the city.

   (b) Dr. Benjamin Spock, who greatly influenced parents' raising of children after World War II, was an _____ pediatrician.

   (c) Dr. Linus Pauling, _____ chemist and winner of two Nobel Prizes, was also an opponent of nuclear weapons testing.

6. **contravene**

   (a) Does it _____ postal regulations to reuse uncancelled stamps?

   (b) I don't mean to _____ you, but I believe you are mistaken.

   (c) We were able to _____ the message before it reached its destination.

7. **emblazon**

   (a) "I never want to speak to you again!" she _____ .

   (b) The French athletes' shirts were _____ with three large red, white, and blue stripes.

   (c) We _____ the words "Go for It" across the twelve-foot banner we hung in the gym.

8. **spry**

   (a) The young dancer's _____ movements endeared her to the audience.

   (b) I noticed the _____ glances they exchanged, and that made me suspicious.

   (c) The _____ heat of the Florida sun wilted the crops.

Fill in the missing word in each sentence. Then write a brief definition of the word. The number in parentheses shows the lesson in which the word appears.

1. The prefix *contra-* (against) and the Latin verb *venire* (to come) combine to form the word _____ (16).

   Definition: _____

2. The prefix *ante-* (before) combines with the Latin *cedere* (to go) form the word _____ (15).

   Definition: _____

3. The Latin *novus* (new) forms the word _____ (16).

   Definition: _____

4. The prefix *bene-* (good) combines with the Latin verb *ficare* (to make) to form the word _____ (10).

   Definition: _____

5. The Latin verb *credere* (to believe) forms the word _____ (12).

   Definition: _____

6. The prefix *magnus* (great) combines with the Latin *animus* (mind; spirit) to form the word _____ (10).

   Definition: _____

7. The Latin verb *tangere* (to touch) forms the word _____ (11).

   Definition: _____

8. The Latin *mater* (mother) forms the word _____ (14).

   Definition: _____

9. The prefix *com-* (with) and the Latin *miser* (wretched) combine to form the word _____ (10).

   Definition: _____

10. The Latin *greg* or *grex* (a flock) forms the word _____ (14).

    Definition: _____

belated

caliber

chagrin

contravene

default

doldrums

emblazon

eminent

expend

expire

exponent

novice

spry

tenuous

truism

Circle the letter of each sentence that suggests the numbered bold vocabulary word. In each group, you may circle more than one letter or none at all.

1. **default**

   (a) The accident couldn't have been prevented, so no one was blamed for it.

   (b) I just can't seem to do anything right around here.

   (c) A tiny flaw in one of the seams caused the metal casing to crack.

2. **expend**

   (a) Riding a bicycle uphill is much harder than going downhill.

   (b) A white dwarf is a star that has no more hydrogen or helium to burn.

   (c) When I take a deep breath, my chest measures forty inches.

3. **novice**

   (a) The first time I tried snowboarding, I felt very nervous.

   (b) Seeing the first crocus after a long winter always cheers me up.

   (c) The first car off the assembly line was a red two-door sports coupe.

4. **chagrin**

   (a) The invitation said formal dress, but Chang arrived in a T-shirt and shorts.

   (b) After boasting that she had an "eagle eye," Joanna missed the target every time.

   (c) There was an awkward silence in the audience as the comedian walked off the stage.

5. **doldrums**

   (a) Those bright specks settling on the bottom of the stream are flecks of gold.

   (b) Business was slack early in the year, and it failed to pick up later.

   (c) Some critics assert that no important poets have emerged in the past twenty years.

6. **caliber**

   (a) How does a .38 Luger differ from a Colt .45 revolver?

   (b) The college accepts only the top five percent of those who apply.

   (c) The measuring instruments are reset each morning to make sure they all agree.

7. **tenuous**

   (a) As long as there was one chance in a million, they would continue to hope for his recovery.

   (b) The new material is said to be ten times stronger than steel.

   (c) His self-confidence, never strong to begin with, has been shattered by his latest test scores.

8. **expire**

   (a) You cannot use this passport after midnight on December 31 of this year.

   (b) Gloria's eyes closed, as though in sleep, for the last time.

   (c) The car stalled so she started the engine again.

9. **spry**

    (a) I suffered minor bruises when I slipped on a sheet of ice.

    (b) The bird was released to the wild after being nursed back to health.

    (c) You can never be sure when she's joking and when she's being serious.

10. **truism**

    (a) I believe her when she says that she was home by ten.

    (b) "What goes up must come down."

    (c) John Adams and Thomas Jefferson both died on July 4, 1826.

16E Passage

Read the passage. Then answer the questions that follow it.

The Marathon

According to legend, the race called the marathon commemorates the feat of a Greek soldier who in 490 B.C.E. ran a distance of 22 miles and 1,470 yards from Marathon to Athens to announce his countrymen's victory over the Persians. Legend also has it that the runner **expired** from exhaustion after achieving his goal. Evidence supporting this story is **tenuous,** however. The first reference to it appeared six hundred years after the event!

Today, in road races throughout the world, the marathon is a popular sporting event. Runners of varying speeds and ability levels enter to test their endurance, break a record, or simply say they had the experience of completing a marathon. A customary part of the modern Olympic games since 1896, the marathon has had a distance of 26 miles and 386 yards since the 1908 Olympics. In that year the race was held in London. It began at the gates of Windsor Castle and ended at the Olympic stadium's royal box, where the king and queen sat.

The 1908 Olympic marathon was memorable for another reason. An American won the gold medal by **default.** The first runner to cross the finish line, an Italian, was **chagrined** to discover that he had been disqualified. British officials had helped him over the last few yards, **contravening** the rule that the runner must complete the full course unaided. After that, an American didn't win again for sixty-four years.

At the 1972 Olympics, Frank Shorter's victory brought the United States' losing streak out of the **doldrums** and significantly increased the popularity of the marathon in the United States. Women's official entry into the sport was **belated;** it was 1972 when they were allowed to enter the Boston Marathon. It wasn't until 1984 that they were allowed to compete in the Olympic event, where they set impressive records of speed. **Eminent** international runners include Grete Waitz of Norway, the predominant female distance runner of the 1970s and 1980s and nine-time winner of the New York City Marathon, and three-time consecutive Boston Marathon winner Uta Pippig of Germany.

belated

caliber

chagrin

contravene

default

doldrums

emblazon

eminent

expend

expire

exponent

novice

spry

tenuous

truism

People of all ages and levels of ability participate in marathons. Those of the highest **caliber** can achieve finishing times of around two and a quarter hours, whereas the goal of a **novice** is often simply to finish. Athletes who are physically challenged are particular **exponents** of the wheelchair competition. Older runners also participate. In the 1991 Boston Marathon, Johnny Kelley, a **spry** 84-year-old, finished in 5 hours, 40 minutes, and 54 seconds. His official number, sixty, **emblazoned** on his shirt, honored the fact that Kelley was competing for the sixtieth time. In 2004, Kelley—then retired—was honored as the race's Grand Marshall. He died later that year. He was 97.

A marathon tests not only powers of physical endurance but also courage and determination. After about twenty miles, long distance runners have **expended** fluids needed by their bodies to supply the muscles with energy. Runners call this "hitting the wall." At this point it is will power more than physical resources that keeps one going to the end of the race. It is a **truism** among runners that anyone can run for twenty miles. But it takes incredible strength to "break the pain barrier."

▶ **Answer each question in the form of a sentence. If a question does not contain a word from the lesson, use one in your answer. Use each word only once.**

1. How can spectators identify runners in a marathon?

   _____

   _____

2. How do runners express an obvious truth about those who finish marathons?

   _____

   _____

3. What was unusual about the American winner of the 1908 Olympic marathon?

   _____

   _____

4. Why couldn't a woman enter the Boston Marathon in 1970?

   _____

   _____

5. How did Frank Shorter's victory in the 1972 Olympics affect the popularity of the marathon in the United States?

   _____

   _____

6. What **eminent** people viewed the 1908 Olympic games?

   _____

   _____

7. What word would you use to describe older marathon runners?

_____

_____

8. Why wouldn't a **novice** runner in a marathon be considered high-**caliber?**

_____

_____

9. What positive claims might a running enthusiast make about distance running?

_____

_____

10. What caused the Greek runner in 490 B.C.E. to **expire?**

_____

_____

FUN & FASCINATING FACTS

- **Doldrums** is a plural noun for which there is no singular. It can take either the singular or plural form of the verb. Originally, a *doldrum* was a dull, apathetic person; the word later lost this meaning and acquired its plural form to describe a depressed or lethargic state of mind. Similarly, light, calm winds occurring north of the equator between the Atlantic and Pacific oceans are called *doldrums*. A person in the *doldrums* probably doesn't have much motivation, just as a ship sailing on the Atlantic or Pacific Ocean doesn't receive much wind from the *doldrums*.

- Don't confuse **eminent** with *imminent,* which means "about to happen." (An important discovery may be *imminent* from such an *eminent* scientist.)

- The Latin *novus* means "new" and forms the root of a number of English words besides **novice.** A *novel* approach to a problem is one that is new; an *innovation* is a new device or new way of doing something; and to *renovate* something is to make it like new again.

belated

caliber

chagrin

contravene

default

doldrums

emblazon

eminent

expend

expire

exponent

novice

spry

tenuous

truism

Hidden Message In the boxes provided, write the words from Lessons 13 through 16 that are missing in each of the sentences. The number following each sentence gives the word list from which the missing word is taken. When the exercise is finished, the shaded boxes should spell out an observation made by Gloria Steinem, twentieth-century American author, journalist, and advocate of women's rights.

1. These recipes will appeal to even the most _____ appetites. **(15)**

2. Boko the clown was famous for his _____ routines. **(14)**

3. When does your driver's license _____? **(16)**

4. The patient consulted the nation's most _____ doctors. **(16)**

5. A kilt is the traditional Scottish _____. **(14)**

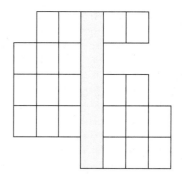

6. I love the cabin's _____ setting by the lake. **(13)**

7. He tried to _____ the speaker by making faces at her. **(13)**

8. The boulder gathered _____ as it rolled downhill. **(15)**

9. Do not _____ the efforts of those trying to help. **(13)**

10. I am willing to _____ assistance to them if they ask. **(13)**

11. A(n) _____ incident marred our visit to Philadelphia. **(13)**

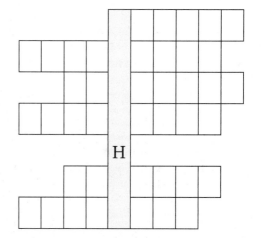

12. They were able to _____ a vast amount of data. **(14)**

13. Spike has the _____ to become a great pitcher. **(15)**

14. You _____ energy whenever you do work. **(16)**

15. The disease could _____ an entire population. **(14)**

16. A(n) _____ eighty-year-old got up and danced a jig. **(16)**

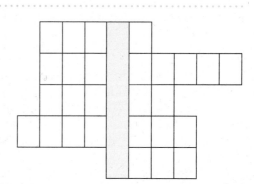

17. The tube was twisted into a(n) _____ shape. **(15)**

18. The Colonial era is _____ to the Federal era. **(15)**

19. One feels a(n) _____ revulsion to acts of cruelty. **(15)**

20. It's useless to _____ with some criminals. **(13)**

21. It's a(n) _____ that "haste makes waste." **(16)**

22. People who are _____ enjoy the company of others. **(14)**

23. The dangers we faced filled me with _____. **(13)**

24. If we have _____ , then we have free will. **(15)**

25. A(n) _____ gets pleasure from being hurt. **(15)**

26. I tried not to _____ on the agreement. **(16)**

27. My _____ aunt is my mother's sister. **(14)**

28. Dr. Selkirk is a(n) _____ of a low-fat diet. **(16)**

29. Her _____ rise to fame astonished her friends. **(13)**

30. I'm not _____ enough to be a juggler. **(14)**

31. To keep the plant healthy, you must _____ it. **(14)**

32. Certain flaws are _____ in the design. **(14)**

33. His _____ behavior soon led to a quarrel. **(14)**

34. She was a(n) _____ at golf, but played well. **(16)**

35. Joe's _____ reply to our question was "Yup." **(13)**

36. Try to _____ the last syllable of the word. **(15)**

37. To my _____, my joke failed to get a laugh. **(16)**

38. He was a good musician but no _____. **(13)**

39. Fuel injection has made carburetors _____. **(15)**

40. Proper training will produce a(n) _____ dog. **(14)**

41. The larger the _____, the bigger the bullet. **(16)**

42. They _____ a different design on each T-shirt. **(16)**

43. The play was a(n) _____ of a Greek tragedy. **(14)**

44. Better a(n) _____ thank-you note than none at all. **(16)**

45. There is a mile-wide _____ on the surface of Mars. **(13)**

46. Despite _____ evidence, the case was soon solved. **(16)**

47. Toy sales are usually in the _____ after the winter holidays. **(16)**

| Word List | Study the definitions of the words. Then do the exercises that follow. |

blight
blīt

n. 1. Any disease that damages plants.
The potato **blight** of the 1840s deprived the Irish people of their main sustenance.

2. Something that harms or destroys.
Dilapidated housing contributes to urban **blight.**

v. To do harm to.
A vote of censure by the United States Senate can **blight** a politician's career.

cite
sīt

v. 1. To mention or quote as an example or authority.
My mother always **cites** *Pride and Prejudice* as a book you can read and enjoy over and over again.

2. To mention for praise.
At an assembly, the principal **cited** Ms. Garcia for her excellent teaching.

3. To summon before a court of law.
Since he was **cited** for speeding last year, my uncle has been a much more prudent driver.

clemency
klem´ ən sē

n. Mercy shown in punishing or judging someone.
When the governor granted his appeal for **clemency,** the ailing prisoner was released from jail.

eccentric
ek sen´ trik

adj. Departing from accepted or normal behavior; odd.
My father was convinced that my brother's tattoos were just another example of his **eccentric** behavior.

n. One who behaves in an odd or peculiar way.
Hetty Green was an **eccentric;** although quite rich, she lived as if she were destitute.

farce
färs

n. 1. A humorous stage play marked by improbable situations and exaggerated behavior.
Charlie Chaplin was the star of *Modern Times*, a hilarious **farce** about technology.

2. An absurd or ridiculous event or situation; a mockery.
The selectmen's meeting turned into a **farce** when every person on the building committee refused to testify and resigned in protest.

foray
fôr´ ā

n. A sudden raid or advance into enemy territory.
The guerrillas left the hills for occasional **forays** into the town to get food.

glean
glēn

v. To gather bit by bit.
President Nelson Mandela's farewell speech to the South African parliament was four and one-half hours long, but I could **glean** its major points from the newspaper the next day.

| **nominal** | *adj.* 1. In name only, not in fact. |
| näm´ ə nəl | The king or queen is the **nominal** head of state in England, but in reality it is the Prime Minister and the Houses of Parliament who rule. |

2. Very small.
The museum charged only a **nominal** entrance fee of fifty cents in order to attract more visitors.

| **ostracize** | *v.* To exclude from a group; to banish. |
| äs´ trə sīz | When the newspaper columnist began writing about the Bavarian town's Nazi past, many of its citizens **ostracized** her. |

| **posthumous** | *adj.* Occurring after a person has died. |
| päs´ tyōo məs | Former slave Johnson Whittaker, expelled from West Point in 1880, was given a **posthumous** commission in the Army 115 years later. |

| **quash** | *v.* 1. To put down by force. |
| kwäsh | British troops tried to **quash** the rebellion of the colonists, but they failed. |

2. To put a stop to legally.
Miners rejoiced when the injunction banning their strike was **quashed** by an appeals court judge.

| **recipient** | *n.* One who receives. |
| rē sip´ ē ənt | Dustin Hoffman has twice been the **recipient** of an Academy Award. |

| **ribald** | *adj.* Funny in a crude way. |
| rib´ əld | Boccaccio was a fourteenth-century Italian writer whose masterpiece, *Decameron*, contained ten **ribald** stories. |

| **suffrage** | *n.* The right to vote. |
| suf´ rij | The twenty-sixth amendment to the Constitution extended **suffrage** to eighteen-year olds. |

| **verve** | *n.* Enthusiasm; vivacity. |
| vʊrv´ | English author Fay Weldon has been writing comic novels with undiminished **verve** for over twenty-five years. |

Read the sentences. If a sentence correctly uses the word in bold, write *C* on the line. If a sentence is incorrect, rewrite it so that the vocabulary word in bold is used correctly.

1. If you **ostracize** someone, you don't have anything to do with that person.

_____

_____

2. A **farce** is a type of play that provokes laughter by its absurdities.

_____

_____

3. A **posthumous** novel is one published after the author's death.

_____

_____

4. **Blight** is a plant disease.

_____

_____

5. **Clemency** is the ability to foretell events.

_____

_____

6. To **quash** an order is to declare that it is no longer in effect.

_____

_____

7. **Verve** is a vague feeling of uneasiness.

_____

_____

8. **Suffrage** is pain or injury caused by another's actions.

_____

_____

9. An **eccentric** is a person who behaves oddly.

_____

_____

10. A **nominal** charge is one that is exorbitant.

_____

_____

11. To make a **foray** into a place is to go in and out quickly.

_____

_____

blight
cite
clemency
eccentric
farce
foray
glean
nominal
ostracize
posthumous
quash
recipient
ribald
suffrage
verve

12. A **ribald** comment is one that is brief and to the point.

_____

_____

13. The **recipient** of something is the immediate cause of it.

_____

_____

14. To **glean** facts is to make them up out of one's head.

_____

_____

15. To be **cited** for good driving is to be commended for it.

_____

_____

17B Using Words

If the word (or a form of the word) in bold fits in a sentence in the group following it, write the word in the blank space. If the word does not fit, leave the space empty. There may be more than one correct answer.

1. **glean**

   (a) I was not able to _____ much information about their intentions from their letter.

   (b) She expects to _____ enough money from the sale of her house to pay her son's college tuition.

   (c) I _____ this antique clock at a flea market in London.

2. **blight**

   (a) Botanists are doing research on the plant virus that causes soybean

   _____ .

   (b) Reports of shark attacks can _____ the tourist industry in a beach resort.

   (c) I hope my having to leave early did not _____ you.

3. **cite**

   (a) He _____ Article One of the Constitution to prove his point.

   (b) Ms. Rosenberg, the principal, _____ my little brother for noticeable improvement in reading.

   (c) We plan to visit the _____ of the ancient city of Troy when we go to Turkey.

4. **ribald**

(a) The young comedian struggled to ignore the audience's _____ remarks.

(b) The pony, a black and white _____ , is very popular with the children on the farm.

(c) The words of the French writer Rabelais (1490–1553) are noted for their _____ humor.

5. **ostracize**

(a) Dr. Haynes _____ the growth on my arm with a special laser.

(b) We _____ the children into three groups for the camping trip.

(c) His racist views were sufficient reason for us to _____ him.

6. **eccentric**

(a) I would hardly call it _____ for a man to part his hair on the side.

(b) The picture above the piano was slightly _____ , so I got up and straightened it.

(c) The writer Gertrude Stein's cigar smoking was considered _____ in Paris in the 1920s.

7. **nominal**

(a) The _____ title of the advocacy group is Students for a Shorter School Day.

(b) In my opinion, ten dollars is not a _____ admission charge!

(c) In math, we learned how to determine the Arabic number that corresponds to any Roman _____ .

8. **farce**

(a) The hero in a _____ is often a clumsy character.

(b) The antics of the Marx Brothers, a comedy trio, made their movie *A Night at the Opera* a hilarious _____ .

(c) The artist took less than fifteen minutes to paint this _____ .

blight
cite
clemency
eccentric
farce
foray
glean
nominal
ostracize
posthumous
quash
recipient
ribald
suffrage
verve

Write the word that makes the most sense in each sentence. Use each word only once. If neither word fits, leave the space blank.

pugnacious / aggressive

1. A(n) _____ manner shows a willingness or eagerness to fight.

2. A good salesperson can be _____ without offending the customer.

3. He pointed a(n) _____ finger at me as he spoke.

clemency / mercy

4. Aunt Lucy showed her _____ in many loving ways.

5. The judge agreed to consider the prisoner's plea for _____.

6. Warrior Genghis Khan showed no _____ to those who opposed him in battle.

novice / beginner

7. A child just learning to read is a _____.

8. After fifty years on the job, it was time for the _____ to retire.

9. After his first year teaching, he was no longer a _____ and was prepared for any challenge.

garb / clothing

10. A bird's _____ is its wings.

11. The store sells _____ for children and adults.

12. The _____ of Stone Age people consisted of animal skins.

disingenuous / insincere

13. The sarcasm of his tone made the words sound _____.

14. While not technically a lie, the statement could certainly be considered _____.

15. Did you notice the _____ way she signs her name?

Circle the letter of each sentence that suggests the numbered bold vocabulary word. In each group, you may circle more than one letter or none at all.

1. **foray**
   (a) The crowd was so excited that they knocked down the fence.
   (b) We met no resistance when our small band rode behind enemy lines.
   (c) Julio took several courses in harmony so he could write music for different instruments.

2. **cite**
   (a) Kaela figured out how to solve the math problem.
   (b) The author gives many examples of cats returning after a long absence.
   (c) The judge carefully explained the charge to the jury.

3. **suffrage**
   (a) The pain from Ranji's broken ankle made it difficult for her to sleep.
   (b) The Nineteenth Amendment, passed in 1920, gave women the right to vote.
   (c) Walking a dog is good exercise for the owner as well as the animal.

4. **verve**
   (a) How dare you take the car without asking permission!
   (b) Someone had left the cap off, and the orange soda had gone flat.
   (c) Winona throws herself wholeheartedly into everything she does.

5. **farce**
   (a) The Morellos were miles from anywhere when their car engine suddenly stopped.
   (b) Patrick declined a third helping of pasta, saying he couldn't eat another thing.
   (c) As Angelo opened the door, the dog ran in, the cat ran out, the newspaper blew away, and the parrot croaked, "Good morning!"

6. **posthumous**
   (a) I saw in the paper that Mr. Poslethwaite died last week.
   (b) The firefighter's widow accepted the medal on her husband's behalf.
   (c) Fame did not come to Kierkegaard, the Danish philosopher, until long after his death.

7. **clemency**
   (a) The jury rejected the death penalty and recommended life imprisonment.
   (b) Calamine lotion always eases the discomfort of my poison ivy.
   (c) Every winter I look forward to eating those delicious little tangerines from Spain.

8. **nominal**
   (a) The numbers 4, 9, 16, and 25 are squares of 2, 3, 4, and 5.
   (b) Perry was supposed to be in charge, but Carin actually ran the gym.
   (c) Sobha's first run around the track was just a warm-up.

blight
cite
clemency
eccentric
farce
foray
glean
nominal
ostracize
posthumous
quash
recipient
ribald
suffrage
verve

9. **recipient**

  (a) Since the letter was addressed to Joanne, I gave it to her right away.

  (b) During Ramadan we always go to the mosque.

  (c) The kindergarten children were thrilled to get six new tricycles for their class.

10. **ostracize**

  (a) Mark suddenly fell silent when Scott's name was mentioned.

  (b) None of the union members would speak to the people who went to work during the miners' strike.

  (c) My new camp T-shirts shrank at least two sizes in the wash.

17E ▶ Passage

Read the passage. Then answer the questions that follow it.

Honor Restored

The United States awards the Congressional Medal of Honor to members of the armed forces for acts of conspicuous bravery in time of war. First issued in 1862, its **recipients** as of 2009 numbered 3,467 men—and one woman.

This woman was Mary Walker, one of the first women doctors in the United States. Born in 1832, Mary Walker gave distinguished service to her country as a Union Army surgeon during the Civil War. Many people believe she also served as a spy for the Union Army; she made frequent **forays** behind enemy lines. Her work was so useful that information she **gleaned** from these ventures saved a Northern army from "a serious reverse," according to one official report. While on one of these missions she was captured by Confederate forces. She spent four months in a Richmond, Virginia, jail, until she was freed as part of a prisoner exchange. In January 1866, President Andrew Johnson awarded Dr. Walker the Medal of Honor, which **cited** her valor on the battlefield in caring for the sick and wounded.

All her life, Dr. Walker was a tireless reformer. She supported female **suffrage** at a time when few women themselves favored the idea. Those who did were regarded by many people as **eccentric.** She was aware of the harmful effects of tobacco; she opposed the habit of smoking. She was opposed to the death penalty, regarding it as barbaric. She also felt that women should not have to wear crinolines, the then fashionable, but uncomfortable, full, stiff skirts supported by "baskets" underneath and puffed out at the back just below the waist by means of pads or a frame. In fact, finding men's clothing both practical and comfortable, Dr. Walker wore it. She thus became a living advertisement for dress reform. Because of this behavior, she was **ostracized** in "polite society." She was sometimes subjected to **ribald** remarks by passers-by. Because she wore men's clothing she was charged with impersonating a man, a punishable offense at the time. She defended herself in court by claiming the right "to dress as I please in free America on whose tented fields I have served for four years in the cause of human freedom." She reminded the court that no one had objected to her wearing the gold-striped trousers of a Union Army officer during the war. After hearing the case, the judge **quashed** the charges and ordered the police to leave her alone. Dr. Walker left the courtroom to the accompaniment of loud applause from the spectators who, while they may have questioned her attire, had nothing but admiration for the **verve** with which she defended her right to dress as she pleased. But public opinion was not always so supportive. Her opposition to capital punishment outraged much of the citizenry when, in 1901, consistent with her beliefs, she circulated an appeal for **clemency** for the murderer of President William McKinley.

In 1917, a military review board examined the cases of everyone who had received the Medal of Honor to ensure that all those who had received the award met the required standards. In the case of Dr. Walker, the board found two deficiencies: first, she was only **nominally** attached to the 52nd Ohio Infantry and not actually a member of the armed forces; and second, although she had performed distinguished service over a period of time, she had not been recognized for a particular act of individual heroism. These facts led the board to ask Dr. Walker to return her medal. Outraged that this repudiation would **blight** her reputation, Dr. Walker's response was, "Over my dead body."

An element of **farce** entered the situation when it was discovered that, through a clerical error, Medals of Honor had been given to all 864 members of the same regiment; in all, 911 medals were recalled. But Dr. Walker found none of this amusing, and although she was breaking the law by doing so, she continued to wear the medal. She died in 1919 as a result of a fall on the Capitol steps. She had gone there in a vain attempt to gain acknowledgment that the medal was rightfully hers.

In the 1970s, Anne Walker, a niece of Dr. Walker, waged a campaign to gain official recognition of her aunt's right to the medal. On June 10, 1977, the Secretary of the Army granted the Congressional Medal of Honor **posthumously** to Dr. Mary Walker, making her once more the only female winner of the nation's highest award for heroism.

▶ **Answer each question in the form of a sentence. If a question does not contain a word from the lesson, use one in your answer. Use each word only once.**

1. What unique distinction does Dr. Mary Walker hold?

_____

_____

2. How was Mary Walker useful to the Union cause?

_____

_____

blight
cite
clemency
eccentric
farce
foray
glean
nominal
ostracize
posthumous
quash
recipient
ribald
suffrage
verve

3. How was the **blight** cast on Dr. Walker's war record finally corrected?

_____

_____

4. Why was Walker summoned before a court of law?

_____

_____

5. What two arguments did Walker make that led the judge to **quash** the charges against her?

_____

_____

6. Why might people consider Walker an early feminist?

_____

_____

7. Why was Walker **ostracized?**

_____

_____

8. How do you think Walker would have responded to **ribald** remarks?

_____

_____

9. What does it mean that Walker was only **nominally** attached to the 52nd Ohio Infantry?

_____

_____

10. Give an example of an unpopular position Walker took that was consistent with her beliefs.

_____

_____

11. How did Walker's **verve** manifest itself throughout her life?

_____

_____

12. What word would you use to describe the situation in which all 864 members of the same regiment received Medals of Honor? How did this happen?

_____

_____

13. Do you think Walker would be considered **eccentric** today? Why or why not?

_____

_____

The Latin *nomen* means "name" and forms the root of a number of English words. A *misnomer* is a name that is improperly applied: for example, calling a whale a fish; to *nominate* someone is to name that person as a candidate for an office; and a **nominal** ruler is one who rules in name only, as did King Victor Emmanuel of Italy in the 1930s, when Mussolini wielded the real power.

In ancient Greece, a citizen of Athens who was deemed dangerous to the state could be banished—sent into exile with no charges brought against him. This happened only to men, since women in ancient Greece were not considered citizens. Citizens voted to banish someone by writing the person's name on a piece of broken pottery or earthenware called an *ostrakon*. If enough votes were cast against the person, he would be **ostracized,** that is, cut off from contact with his fellow citizens. The word has passed unchanged in form and meaning to the present day.

blight

cite

clemency

eccentric

farce

foray

glean

nominal

ostracize

posthumous

quash

recipient

ribald

suffrage

verve

For more practice and games, go to www.WordlyWise3000.com.

Lesson 18

Word List

Study the definitions of the words. Then do the exercises that follow.

adhere
ad hir´

v. 1. To stick to; stay attached.
I had to use tape to make sure the stamp **adhered** to the envelope.

2. To follow closely or faithfully.
Millions of people in India still **adhere** to the nonviolent principles of Gandhi, the Hindu leader who died in 1948.

adherence *n.*
The Amish are a sect that are known for their **adherence** to a simple lifestyle that rejects cars, for example, preferring horses and carriages.

adherent *n.* A follower or supporter of an idea.
The proposal to eliminate the theater program has few **adherents,** so Mr. Speca is averse to going ahead with it.

aplomb
ə pläm´

n. Complete self-confidence and poise.
Although she was nervous, the thirteen-year-old gymnast shook hands with the president with the **aplomb** of a diplomat.

brandish
bran´ dish

v. To shake or wave in a threatening way.
Even though she would never hurt her little brother, Katharine would **brandish** her fist at him in an attempt to intimidate him.

broach
brōch

v. To bring up for discussion; to begin to talk about.
Rosa decided to wait until after dinner to **broach** the subject of an increase in her allowance.

devotee
dev ə tā´

n. An ardent follower, supporter, or enthusiast.
Julius is a **devotee** of Gilbert and Sullivan; his favorite operetta is "Ruddigore."

diffident
dif´ i dənt

adj. Unsure of oneself; shy; reserved in manner.
Even though he was a world-renowned pianist, Rudolf Serkin had a **diffident** manner.

diffidence *n.*
When he walked onto the stage, his shy smile and head tilted to one side testified to his **diffidence.**

extravaganza
ek strav´ ə gan´ zə

n. An elaborate and spectacular display or event.
The opening ceremony of the 2004 Olympic Games in Athens, Greece, was an **extravaganza** watched on television by millions all over the world.

integrity in teg´ rə tē	*n.* 1. Honesty; trustworthiness. People may not have agreed with the governor's political views, but no one questioned her **integrity.** 2. The condition of being whole or complete. My English teacher disapproves of rewriting a published book to make it easier to read because he says it violates the **integrity** of the work.
plaintive plān´ tiv	*adj.* Expressing sorrow; mournful. We finally brought in the dog because his **plaintive** whining was making us feel bad.
plaudit plôd´ ət	*n.* (usually plural) A demonstration of strong approval or praise. The ice skater raised her arms and bowed slightly to acknowledge the **plaudits** of the crowd.
regalia ri gāl´ yə	*n. pl.* The symbols, objects, or special costumes worn by or associated with a group; special clothing. The guards at Buckingham Palace, in London, are in full **regalia** as they march back and forth.
resplendent rə splen´ dənt	*adj.* Dazzling in appearance. My grandmother was **resplendent** in a dress of burgundy velvet at her ninetieth birthday party.
subordinate sə bôrd´ n ət	*adj.* Less important; secondary. The actress Emma Thompson said she would willingly take a **subordinate** role in a play if she found the character interesting. *n.* A person under the command or control of another. The general had a reputation for being unusually fair and respectful to his **subordinates.** *v.* (sə bôrd´ n āt) To give less importance to; to place in a lesser position. Sometimes parents have to **subordinate** their own interests to those of their children.
surmount sər mount´	*v.* To defeat or overcome. With the help of Anne Sullivan, Helen Keller was able to **surmount** devastating physical problems.
tenable ten´ ə bəl	*adj.* Capable of being defended; reasonable. Sebastian was such an effective debater that he could argue a position that at first did not seem at all **tenable,** and then be utterly convincing.

Read the sentences. If a sentence correctly uses the word in bold, write *C* on the line. If a sentence is incorrect, rewrite it so that the vocabulary word in bold is used correctly.

1. To **broach** a topic is to introduce it into a conversation.

   _____

   _____

2. A **devotee** is a person who shuns the company of older people.

   _____

   _____

3. A person of **integrity** is someone whose word can be relied on.

   _____

   _____

4. A **tenable** position is one that is reasonable.

   _____

   _____

5. **Plaudits** are insults hurled at someone to express displeasure.

   _____

   _____

6. To **adhere** to a surface is to stick to it.

   _____

   _____

7. To do something with **aplomb** is to do it with assurance.

   _____

   _____

8. To be **subordinate** is to be under the authority of another.

   _____

   _____

9. To **surmount** an obstacle is to avoid it completely.

   _____

   _____

10. A **diffident** manner is one that lacks conviction or confidence.

    _____

    _____

11. To be **resplendent** is to be dressed in splendid garb.

    _____

    _____

12. A **plaintive** sound is one that stays on the same level for a long time.

_____

_____

13. An **extravaganza** is an item that costs more than one can afford.

_____

_____

14. **Regalia** is the bearing of oneself with dignity.

_____

_____

15. To **brandish** a weapon is to wield it as if you were going to use it.

_____

_____

18B Using Words

If the word (or a form of the word) in bold fits in a sentence in the group following it, write the word in the blank space. If the word does not fit, leave the space empty. There may be more than one correct answer.

1. **extravaganza**

(a) *Phantom of the Opera* is a multimillion dollar Broadway _____ .

(b) Having five homes seems like a needless _____ .

(c) A gaudily decorated _____ led the Thanksgiving Day parade down New York's Fifth Avenue.

2. **brandish**

(a) We _____ our arms frantically to attract the usher's attention.

(b) The letters UCLA were _____ across the quarterback's sweatshirt.

(c) The farmer _____ his walking stick at us and told us to stay off places that were seeded.

3. **adhere**

(a) The wallpaper won't _____ to the wall if the paste is too powdery.

(b) She _____ to her political beliefs even though her family strongly disagreed with her.

(c) The president promised to _____ to his candidate for the post in spite of congressional opposition.

adhere

aplomb

brandish

broach

devotee

diffident

extravaganza

integrity

plaintive

plaudit

regalia

resplendent

subordinate

surmount

tenable

4. **subordinate**

(a) In the Middle Ages, most lords were unwilling to _____ their privileges to the improvement of their serfs' lives.

(b) Because he occupied a _____ position in the company, the intern was docile and quiet.

(c) If a lawyer _____ perjury, she can be called before the Bar Association.

5. **broach**

(a) The socialite thought that wearing a _____ in the shape of a dollar sign was in bad taste.

(b) The water was pouring through a _____ in the dam.

(c) My grandfather changed the subject just as I was about to _____ the topic of his retirement.

6. **plaudit**

(a) The crowd waved colorful _____ as they greeted the candidate.

(b) The new version of Hugo's *Les Miserables* garnered _____ from critics.

(c) The only _____ I received after I gave my report was a note from the librarian asking me to return my books.

7. **resplendent**

(a) The Senegalese choir was _____ in their brightly patterned robes.

(b) My grandparents had a _____ time in Disney World, staying for a week.

(c) The waitress beamed when she saw the _____ tip Elena left.

8. **tenable**

(a) The general withdrew from the battle when he saw his position was no longer

_____ .

(b) Ann thinks so fast on her feet that she can make any position seem _____ .

(c) The warranty on my new car is _____ for five years or fifty thousand miles.

18C Word Study

Each group of words contains two words that are either synonyms or antonyms. Circle them. Then circle *S* if they are synonyms or *A* if they are antonyms.

1. detach	enlarge	brandish	adhere	S	A
2. diffident	vociferous	belated	centrifugal	S	A

3. resplendent	eminent	drab	tenuous	S	A
4. eccentric	jaded	ribald	cynical	S	A
5. clemency	adherence	aplomb	severity	S	A
6. plaudit	devotee	aficionado	novice	S	A
7. momentum	indolence	potential	verve	S	A
8. truism	recipient	donor	exponent	S	A
9. tenuous	obsolescent	firm	diffident	S	A
10. contravene	accentuate	surmount	disobey	S	A

18D Images of Words

Circle the letter of each sentence that suggests the numbered bold vocabulary word. In each group, you may circle more than one letter or none at all.

adhere
aplomb
brandish
broach
devotee
diffident
extravaganza
integrity
plaintive
plaudit
regalia
resplendent
subordinate
surmount
tenable

1. **integrity**
   (a) When my mother makes you a promise, you know you can count on it.
   (b) The Roman Empire collapsed because of its own internal weaknesses.
   (c) In David Copperfield, Uriah Heep works his way from the position of clerk to partner in a law office.

2. **broach**
   (a) Thien couldn't stop talking about how thrilled he was to come in first in the 100-yard dash.
   (b) When the personnel manager had finished describing the job, Alison decided to bring up the issue of salary.
   (c) Ruth gasped when, after a long silence, Antonio said he was thinking of selling the store.

3. **subordinate**
   (a) I thought it was only polite to take the smaller of the two pieces of cake Nabil offered me.
   (b) Even though I was upset about forgetting several notes of my piece, I managed to take a bow and smile at the audience.
   (c) Prices on running shoes have been cut by twenty percent for the end-of-winter sale.

4. surmount

(a) Despite losing a knight and a rook, Kasparov was able to win the chess match.

(b) There is a five-dollar additional charge for overnight delivery.

(c) Mr. Darcy was able to climb easily into the saddle and ride off.

5. aplomb

(a) A line with a lead weight on the end shows you if the line is vertical.

(b) I was in the audience and never suspected that Marco had forgotten his lines and was making them up.

(c) Despite the power failure that silenced her microphone, the speaker moved closer to the audience and finished the rest of her speech.

6. diffidence

(a) I'm not sure I deserve the award for most helpful student.

(b) Cherest never expresses an opinion about a controversial issue until he has read all about it.

(c) It doesn't matter to me whether we have rice or potatoes with the fish.

7. plaintive

(a) When the Irish tenor John McCormack sang those songs of lost love, it brought tears to my eyes.

(b) The judge assigned a new young lawyer to the property dispute.

(c) Eve asked the waiter to take back her beef because it was undercooked.

8. adhere

(a) There must have been a hundred people jammed into the hot subway car at rush hour.

(b) Line the pan with waxed paper so the cake batter won't stick to the bottom.

(c) Aurelia has been a devout believer in homeopathy since her persistent sore throat was cured by one of its remedies.

9. regalia

(a) The Surgeon General was never seen in public without his officer's uniform and all his medals.

(b) The sailboats were lined up at the pier for the start of the race.

(c) We were having so much fun that we wanted the graduation party to go on forever.

10. devotee

(a) Ezra has read every novel by S. E. Hinton at least six times.

(b) When all the ballots were counted, the seven members of the school committee were reelected.

(c) His fans were very upset by the death of the Grateful Dead's Jerry Garcia.

Read the passage. Then answer the questions that follow it.

The American Indian Dance Theater

Hanay Geiogamah (Hə nā´ Gig´ ə mə) was a **devotee** of Native American Dance. A member of the Kiowa/Delaware tribe of Oklahoma, with a professional interest in theater, he believed that the dances of the American Indians, an essential part of their lives, could and should be introduced to a wider audience. He **broached** the idea of forming a Native American dance company to Barbara Schwei, a New York concert producer. She agreed with Geiogamah. The two began traveling to competitions held at tribal gatherings throughout the western United States in order to recruit dancers.

There was some doubt at first about whether the idea was **tenable.** Many of the dancers they approached were **diffident** about becoming entertainers and performing in public. In addition, many of the dances they performed had been passed down from generation to generation and were sacred to the tribe; they could not be performed without the permission of the tribal elders. Geiogamah and Schwei managed to **surmount** these problems, and they offered reassurance that the **integrity** of the dances would be respected.

In the spring of 1987, they assembled a group of dancers in Colorado and launched the American Indian Dance Theater. The company was made up of twenty-four dancers from twenty different tribes from across the United States and Canada. The dancers varied greatly in the ways they moved. Yet they performed each other's dances and sang each other's songs. The dances ranged from those of the Kwakwak'wakw peoples of the northwest coast of British Columbia to competitions between men in ornate feathered costumes or women in elegant shawls. Within two years, the company had won **plaudits** from the critics and was being enthusiastically received throughout the country. The performers accepted their rise to fame with **aplomb.** The company went on to tour Europe, the Middle East, North Africa, South America, and Australia.

Those fortunate enough to see a performance of the American Indian Dance Theater experience an **extravaganza** of color, often-whirling motion, and tribal music. In full **regalia,** the dancers are **resplendent** in colorful masks and costumes decorated with beads, feathers, fringes, and ornaments of precious metals. Company members and their families make all the elaborate masks, jewelry, and costumes themselves. Some of the materials the dancers wear have special meaning: angora goat hair, for example, used in leggings, represents surefootedness, while eagle feathers stand for power and bravery.

The eagle, believed to be a messenger between the spirit realm and humankind, is sacred to all tribes. It is featured in many of the dances. There is a stately Eagle Dance, performed by Zunis of New Mexico. Another, danced by Plains Indians, acts out the bird's life cycle to the accompaniment of the **plaintive** music of a wooden

adhere

aplomb

brandish

broach

devotee

diffident

extravaganza

integrity

plaintive

plaudit

regalia

resplendent

subordinate

surmount

tenable

flute. The Apache Crown Dance comes from another ancient tribal ceremony, in which performers **brandish** symbolic wands that heal the sick while a clown dances among them all, offering comic relief.

Geiogamah and Schwei have departed from tradition in one important respect. Women played a **subordinate** role in Native American dance, but not in the American Indian Dance Theater. Female dancers play a prominent part in the company. They are featured in the colorful Butterfly, Fancy Shawl, and other dances. "The role of women has changed," Geiogamah, the artistic director explains, "and it's necessary for us to reflect the change in the flow of life." What has not changed is the company's strict **adherence** to the form and the significance of traditional Native American dances.

▶ **Answer each question in the form of a sentence. If a question does not contain a word from the lesson, use one in your answer. Use each word only once.**

1. Why did Geiogamah **broach** the subject of starting a Native American dance company to Barbara Schwei?

   _____

   _____

2. Why might Barbara Schwei have been **diffident** about Geiogamah's idea at first?

   _____

   _____

3. Why do Geiogamah and Schwei deserve **plaudits?**

   _____

   _____

4. How was the **integrity** of the traditional Native American dances preserved?

   _____

   _____

5. What makes the show an **extravaganza?**

   _____

   _____

6. Why are American Indians **devotees** of the eagle?

   _____

   _____

7. Why might the clowns have to dodge during the Apache Crown Dance?

   _____

   _____

8. Do you think the dancers were dismayed by the company's success?

_____

_____

9. What suggests that the Eagle Dance performed by the Plains Indians is sad?

_____

_____

10. In what important respect has the Dance Theater not **adhered** to tradition?

_____

_____

FUN & FASCINATING FACTS

A person showing **aplomb** is not easily thrown off balance, as the origin of the word suggests. *Aplomb* comes from the Latin *plumbum,* "lead." As you learned in Lesson 1, a line with a lead weight on the end is called a *plumb* line; it is not easily disturbed or moved from its position at rest because lead is such a heavy metal.

The Latin verb *tenere* means "to hold"; it forms the root of a number of English words. A *tenacious* person is one who holds on to something and is unwilling to let go. The *tenor* of an argument or discussion is the main point that is held throughout it. Finally, a **tenable** position is one that can be held with some confidence because it is reasonable and has a solid basis.

adhere

aplomb

brandish

broach

devotee

diffident

extravaganza

integrity

plaintive

plaudit

regalia

resplendent

subordinate

surmount

tenable

Lesson 19

Word List	Study the definitions of the words. Then do the exercises that follow.

apex
ā´ peks

n. The highest point of something.
Visitors can climb to the **apex** of the temple of the sun, a pyramid in Mexico.

collusion
kə lōō´ zhən

n. A secret agreement between parties for a criminal or deceitful purpose.
The four companies were cited for acting in **collusion** to fix prices illegally.

incinerate
in sin´ ər āt´

v. To burn to ashes.
Before recycling became the norm, we used to **incinerate** all our old newspapers in the furnace.

indict
in dīt´

v. To charge with a crime.
After a preliminary hearing, the defendant was **indicted** for shoplifting.

indictment *n.*
In 1971, a grand jury brought an **indictment** against several top-level officials in the Watergate scandal.

judicial
jōō dish´ əl

adj. Having to do with judges, the law, or the courts.
Standard **judicial** attire in the United States is a long black robe.

martyr
märt´ ər

n. One who chooses to suffer or die rather than give up beliefs or principles.
Joan of Arc was the French **martyr** burned at the stake by the English in 1431.

v. To be put to death for one's beliefs.
Christians in ancient Rome were **martyred** for their religious beliefs by being thrown to the lions.

multitude
mul´ tə tōōd

n. 1. A large number of people or things.
This report on global warming covers a **multitude** of topics.

2. A large group of people; a crowd.
Helicopters flew overhead as the president addressed the **multitude.**

rescind
rē sind´

v. To do away with; to cancel.
The Citadel, a South Carolina military college, **rescinded** its ban on admitting women following a court order in 1995.

revere
rē vir´

v. To have great respect and affection for.
His contemporaries **revered** George Washington for his character and leadership.

scion
sī´ ən

n. 1. A descendant or heir.
Britain's Prince Charles is a **scion** of the House of Windsor.

2. A cutting from a plant used to produce new growth.
The **scions** you grafted onto the apple trees should produce fruit in three years.

sordid sôr´ did	*adj.* Dirty or disgusting. The **sordid** details of the senator's bribe-taking were revealed in his diary.
suave swäv´	*adj.* Smoothly polite; blandly pleasing. She had such a **suave** demeanor that she charmed almost everyone she met.
travesty trav´ əs tē	*n.* A distorted example or imitation. Some news stations turn the reporting of world events into a **travesty** of responsible journalism.
vindicate vin´ də kāt	*v.* 1. To free from blame, guilt, or suspicion. The suspect was released when an eyewitness came forward with testimony to **vindicate** him. 2. To show to be true or right. The company was asked to **vindicate** its claim that its products were safe.
vitriolic vi´ trē äl´ ik	*adj.* Having a sharp, biting quality; bitterly sarcastic. I concluded from the **vitriolic** Boston reviews that the play would not make it to Broadway.

 19A   Understanding Meanings

Read the sentences. If a sentence correctly uses the word in bold, write *C* on the line. If a sentence is incorrect, rewrite it so that the vocabulary word in bold is used correctly.

1. To **rescind** an offer is to withdraw it.

_____

_____

2. A **martyr** is a person who subjects others to harsh treatment.

_____

_____

3. **Collusion** is an underhanded collaboration.

_____

_____

4. To **vindicate** something is to conquer it.

_____

_____

apex
collusion
incinerate
indict
judicial
martyr
multitude
rescind
revere
scion
sordid
suave
travesty
vindicate
vitriolic

5. A **scion** is a shoot from a plant that can be grafted onto another plant.

_____

_____

6. A **multitude** is a gathering of many people.

_____

_____

7. To **revere** someone is to take revenge on that person.

_____

_____

8. An **indictment** is a legal accusation of wrongdoing.

_____

_____

9. A **sordid** crime is one that is especially evil or reprehensible.

_____

_____

10. A **judicial** decision is one that can be enforced by the court.

_____

_____

11. To **incinerate** something is to suggest it without offering proof.

_____

_____

12. A **suave** person is one who makes promises and doesn't keep them.

_____

_____

13. The **apex** is the top of something.

_____

_____

14. A **vitriolic** statement is one that can express angry criticism.

_____

_____

15. A **travesty** is a way of crossing from one side to the other.

_____

_____

If the word (or a form of the word) in bold fits in a sentence in the group following it, write the word in the blank space. If the word does not fit, leave the space empty. There may be more than one correct answer.

1. **vindicate**

   (a) Admitting that you did wrong does not _____ you.

   (b) Please _____ the location of your house on this map.

   (c) De Gaulle's aim was to _____ France's honor after the Nazi invasion.

2. **martyr**

   (a) The slain Malcolm X was mourned as a _____ by his followers.

   (b) Some religions venerate _____ saints.

   (c) Thousands of civilians were _____ in the Balkan wars of the 1990s.

3. **multitude**

   (a) A great _____ gathered to hear Janis Joplin sing.

   (b) She had a _____ of excuses for not cleaning up after dinner.

   (c) A vast _____ of stars stood out against the velvety blackness of the sky.

4. **collusion**

   (a) The police believe the two brothers acted in _____ to rob the bank.

   (b) The _____ occurred when the truck failed to stop at a red light.

   (c) Suspected _____ between drug dealers and some police officers is under investigation.

5. **scion**

   (a) The _____ containing buds was grafted onto the root stock of the tree.

   (b) Prince William and Prince Harry are _____ of the royal family in England.

   (c) A mare's _____ is called a foal.

6. **suave**

   (a) In winter, she wore a _____ wool coat that reached her ankles.

   (b) The _____ actor starred in a series of light comedies.

   (c) His _____ manner carried him through many difficult situations.

apex
collusion
incinerate
indict
judicial
martyr
multitude
rescind
revere
scion
sordid
suave
travesty
vindicate
vitriolic

7. **indict**

  (a) There were fourteen charges in the _____ handed down by the grand jury.

  (b) The district attorney has plenty of evidence to _____ the gang members.

  (c) The bus driver didn't _____ whether she would be taking on additional passengers.

8. **rescind**

  (a) The company agreed to _____ the order requiring overtime work.

  (b) I told the server I wished to _____ my original order because I wanted chili instead.

  (c) The blizzard forced the sporting goods store to _____ its super sale.

19c ▷ Word Study

Complete the analogies by selecting the pair of words whose relationship most resembles the relationship of the pair in capital letters. Circle the letter in front of the pair you choose.

1. ASHES : INCINERATE ::
  (a) melt : ice
  (b) toast : burn
  (c) smoke : rise
  (d) ice : freeze

2. BLIGHT : DAMAGE ::
  (a) measles : disease
  (b) hospital : doctor
  (c) bark : tree
  (d) cure : recovery

3. NOMINAL : SUBSTANTIAL ::
  (a) articulate : speaking
  (b) widespread : ubiquitous
  (c) small : large
  (d) trite : facetious

4. MULTITUDE : MANY ::
  (a) pair : two
  (b) paucity : none
  (c) size : small
  (d) jungle : sylvan

5. DIFFIDENT : OVERBEARING ::
  (a) harrowing : traumatic
  (b) belated : posthumous
  (c) haphazard : convoluted
  (d) nondescript : flamboyant

6. MEDAL : REGALIA ::
  (a) hubbub : riot
  (b) facet : visage
  (c) plaudit : lament
  (d) mask : costume

7. JUDICIAL : JUDGE ::
  (a) gratis : price
  (b) royal : monarch
  (c) studious : student
  (d) incontrovertible : fact

8. APLOMB : SUAVE ::
   (a) alacrity : fast
   (b) integrity : disingenuous
   (c) fear : brave
   (d) chagrin : idyllic

9. APEX : ZENITH ::
   (a) time : clock
   b) facet : face
   (c) verve : indolence
   (d) circle : center

10. DESPISE : REVERE ::
    (a) garner : glean
    (b) accentuate : emphasize
    (c) give : receive
    (d) regret : lament

19D Images of Words

Circle the letter of each sentence that suggests the numbered bold vocabulary word. In each group, you may circle more than one letter or none at all.

1. **judicial**
   (a) A judge's decisions are subject to review by a higher court.
   (b) A series of wise business decisions made Gladys a rich woman.
   (c) The legal system in Louisiana differs from that of other states.

2. **apex**
   (a) The Washington Monument is about 555 feet tall.
   (b) The Japanese writer Yasunari Kawabata won the Nobel Prize in Literature in 1968.
   (c) Jackie Joyner-Kersee holds the world's record in the heptathlon.

3. **vitriolic**
   (a) The author felt devastated when he read the critic's nasty review.
   (b) Carmen ran for ice cubes when boiling water splashed her hand.
   (c) The teacher evaluated her students with a written report.

4. **revere**
   (a) Once she had let the car warm up, she backed out of the driveway.
   (b) Sue was quite fond of her grandmother and visited her as often as possible.
   (c) Martin Luther King Jr. was held in high esteem by many people.

5. **incinerate**
   (a) The sand was so hot under the blazing sun that it hurt our bare feet.
   (b) The forest fire left not a tree standing for miles around.
   (c) Several tons of garbage were reduced to ashes each day by the town.

6. **sordid**
   (a) Willie admitted returning his library books late.
   (b) The immigrants were virtually imprisoned in the crumbling brick factory.
   (c) Some tabloid newspapers revel in printing sensational details of celebrities' private lives.

apex
collusion
incinerate
indict
judicial
martyr
multitude
rescind
revere
scion
sordid
suave
travesty
vindicate
vitriolic

7. **martyr**

   (a) Charles Dickens died in 1870 at the age of 58.

   (b) Millions died from smallpox before a vaccine was discovered to combat the disease.

   (c) President Lincoln was fatally shot by a man who opposed his politics, as he watched a play at Ford's Theater.

8. **travesty**

   (a) The guilt of the defendants had been decided before the "trial" began.

   (b) A musical version of *Macbeth*, set in Las Vegas, closed after just one night.

   (c) "This season's television sitcoms are the worst in many years," the writer said.

9. **collusion**

   (a) William Gilbert and Arthur Sullivan worked together on many operettas.

   (b) The gatekeeper admitted giving the thieves a key to the warehouse.

   (c) The airline was known for losing people's luggage.

10. **scion**

    (a) The healthy shoot is inserted into a slit cut in the rootstock.

    (b) Prince Hal was the son of Henry IV and succeeded him as king.

    (c) Emperor penguins warm the eggs they lay by holding them atop their feet and hunching over them.

 **19E** Passage

Read the passage. Then answer the questions that follow it.

A Controversial Prime Minister

On December 1, 1988, Benazir Bhutto, aged 35, was sworn in as prime minister of Pakistan. She was the first woman in modern times ever to be elected the head of state in a Muslim country. Bhutto reached the **apex** of political power, a remarkable feat in a country whose culture is dominated by men. Her election **vindicated** the honor of her father, the former Prime Minister Zulfikar Ali Bhutto. Ten years earlier, he had been taken prisoner and ordered executed by the military ruler General Zia after a trial that Benazir Bhutto condemned as a **travesty** of justice.

Benazir Bhutto grew up a child of privilege. Her father, an Oxford-educated lawyer, the **scion** of a wealthy and influential family, was drawn into politics at an early age. Following the defeat of Pakistan in its 1971 war with India, the **suave** diplomat-turned-politician and founder of the Pakistan People's Party (PPP) was first appointed president. Then, under a new constitution, he was officially elected prime minister. He encountered opposition almost immediately when he began the difficult task of cleaning up Pakistan's **sordid** political system, which was run by the military in **collusion** with some of the country's elite families.

Her autobiography, *Daughter of Destiny*, suggests that Benazir Bhutto **revered** her father, and that he, in turn, idolized her. Taking her into his confidence, he introduced her to many world leaders and sent her to Radcliffe and Oxford to study government. In 1977, having completed her studies, she returned to Pakistan. She scarcely had time to unpack before General Zia, the army chief of staff, overthrew her father in a military coup. Shortly thereafter, Zia had him **indicted** on charges of ordering the assassination of a political opponent. Despite appeals from world leaders, her father was executed. It was an act she considers **judicial** murder. Benazir Bhutto and her mother were then placed under house arrest.

The eleven-year rule of General Zia was marked by the brutal suppression of civil liberties. The PPP was outlawed. When supporters of the **martyred** Bhutto demonstrated, they were tear-gassed, arrested, and clubbed. Benazir Bhutto felt that the torch of leadership had been passed to her, and her **vitriolic** expression of contempt for General Zia led to her imprisonment. In 1981 she was held in solitary confinement for five months, with no toilet or running water. During this time, she was denied medical treatment. Her guards would sometimes leave a bottle of poison in her cell.

General Zia failed to break her spirit, however. In 1984 she was permitted to leave the country; she chose to settle in London. Two years later, responding to international pressure, General Zia **rescinded** his ban on political parties. Bhutto was allowed to return to Pakistan. She went on a triumphant tour of the country, greeted by **multitudes** of joyous PPP supporters. In August 1988, a plane carrying Zia and his top military advisers crashed, **incinerating** everyone aboard.

Several months later, Benazir Bhutto led the PPP to victory. She held the office of prime minister for two years, restoring civil liberties and releasing political prisoners. She faced political opposition at every turn, and was even forced to combat charges of corruption within her own administration. Though her narrow reelection in 1993 secured her place in office for a few years, Benazir Bhutto lost the race for prime minister in 1997. The military quickly overthrew the newly elected government and Bhutto was exiled from her own country. In the fall of 2007, Bhutto returned to Pakistan to continue her struggle against the country's corrupt political system. Her battle came to a tragic end on December 27, 2007, when she was assassinated at a political rally in Pakistan. Like her father before her, Bhutto gave her life fighting to do what was best for her country and its people.

▶ **Answer each question in the form of a sentence. If a question does not contain a word from the lesson, use one in your answer. Use each word only once.**

1. What attributes suited Zulfikar Bhutto for diplomacy?

_____

_____

apex
collusion
incinerate
indict
judicial
martyr
multitude
rescind
revere
scion
sordid
suave
travesty
vindicate
vitriolic

2. What happened to Zulfikar Bhutto when he refused to act in **collusion** with the military?

_____

_____

3. How did Benazir Bhutto view her father's trial and execution?

_____

_____

4. What was a result of Benazir Bhutto's resistance to General Zia?

_____

_____

5. Describe the conditions of Benazir Bhutto's prison cell.

_____

_____

6. How does the author of the passage show that people **revered** Benazir Bhutto?

_____

_____

7. Why was Benazir Bhutto able to run for office after her return from exile?

_____

_____

8. What happened to General Zia's plane?

_____

_____

9. How was Zulfikar Bhutto's faith in his daughter's abilities **vindicated?**

_____

_____

10. Why is Zulfikar Bhutto described as Pakistan's **martyred** leader?

_____

_____

11. At the end of the passage, is Benazir Bhutto's political career at its **apex?** Why or why not?

_____

_____

Don't confuse **judicial** with *judicious,* which means "wise; carefully thought out." A *judicial* decision is one made by a judge or a court of law; it may or may not be *judicious*. Both words are formed from the Latin *iudic,* "judge."

Martyr comes from the Greek *martus,* which means "witness." It originally referred to persons who bore witness to their beliefs by being willing to die for them. Such persons could have escaped death by denying their beliefs, but refused to do so. *Martyr* has acquired broader meanings over the centuries and can refer to persons who are murdered or unjustly put to death. It can also be applied to one who suffers over a long period, but bears pain without complaining.

Sulfuric acid is one of the most destructive substances known. It will burn, corrode, or dissolve its way through any container in which it is placed, with few exceptions. One of the materials that can withstand its corrosiveness is glass. Another name for sulfuric acid is oil of vitriol. A **vitriolic** attack on someone is one that is vicious or destructive, and invites comparison to the corrosive qualities of sulfuric acid.

apex

collusion

incinerate

indict

judicial

martyr

multitude

rescind

revere

scion

sordid

suave

travesty

vindicate

vitriolic

Lesson **20**

For more practice and games, go
to **www.WordlyWise3000.com**.

Word List	Study the definitions of the words. Then do the exercises that follow.

bogus
bō´gəs

adj. Counterfeit or fake.
The art historian discovered a **bogus** Rembrandt hanging in the museum.

demise
di mīz´

n. The end of existence or activity; death.
Mark Twain wryly observed that reports of his **demise** were greatly exaggerated.

devise
di vīz´

v. To form or arrange in the mind.
The personnel manager had to **devise** a training program for all the new workers.

enshrine
ən shrīn´

v. To cherish as precious or sacred.
The Vietnam Memorial, in Washington, D.C., helps **enshrine** the memory of those who died in the Vietnam War.

evince
ē vins´

v. 1. To show clearly; to express.
Julio **evinces** his talent for baking with his delicious cookies.

2. To provoke.
The comedian's zany antics failed to **evince** a laugh from his audience.

irrevocable
ir rev´ ə kə bəl

adj. Impossible to change.
Your birthday is an **irrevocable** fact of life.

martial
mär´ shəl

adj. Having to do with war, armies, or fighting.
Karate and judo are two of the **martial** arts.

memorabilia
mem´ ər ə bil´ ē ə

n. pl. Objects collected over a period of time that recall particular events.
Thomas Edison's **memorabilia** can be seen at his winter home in Fort Myers, Florida.

mundane
mun dān´

adj. Of or relating to ordinary, everyday matters.
Checking a report for spelling errors is a **mundane** but necessary task.

patronize
pā´ trə nīz

v. 1. To be a supporter or regular customer of.
I **patronize** the downtown stores rather than the ones at the new mall.

2. To treat in a condescending way.
"I am not your dear young lady," she remonstrated, "and please don't **patronize** me by addressing me that way."

| querulous | *adj.* Apt to find fault; complaining. |
| kwer´ ə ləs | I commiserated with him for having to put up with his visiting uncle's **querulous** demands. |

quirk	*n.* 1. A peculiar or eccentric mannerism.
kwʉrk	Signing his letters "Your obedient servant" is one of his **quirks.**
	2. An odd or sudden turn of events.
	A **quirk** of fate brought us both to the spot where we had first met ten years earlier.

| refute | *v.* To prove to be false; to disprove. |
| rē fyo͞ot´ | I **refuted** her claim that taking vitamins was a waste of time by showing her the latest research from the medical group. |

sanction	*n.* 1. Approval or permission from an authority.
saŋk´ shən	The principal gave her **sanction** for the establishment of a student council.
	2. An action taken by one nation against another.
	Economic **sanctions** against South Africa were lifted when it ended its policy of apartheid.
	v. To approve or allow.
	The United States government refused to **sanction** travel to Cuba as long as Castro was in power.

| tome | *n.* A book, especially one that is large. |
| tōm | I admired the **tome's** sumptuous satiny jacket, but had trouble wading through its twelve hundred pages. |

20A ▶ Understanding Meanings

Read the sentences. If a sentence correctly uses the word in bold, write *C* on the line. If a sentence is incorrect, rewrite it so that the vocabulary word in bold is used correctly.

1. **Memorabilia** are reminders of events that occurred long before.

   _____

   _____

2. A **martial** song is peaceful and soothing.

   _____

   _____

3. A **querulous** customer is difficult to satisfy.

   _____

   _____

4. **Mundane** matters are those one has difficulty understanding.

_____

_____

5. To **sanction** an activity is to permit it.

_____

_____

6. A **bogus** report is one that is not genuine.

_____

_____

7. An **irrevocable** agreement is one that cannot be terminated.

_____

_____

8. A person's **demise** is the property left after her or his death.

_____

_____

9. To **devise** a solution is to pass it off falsely as one's own.

_____

_____

10. A **quirk** is an odd way of doing something.

_____

_____

11. A **tome** is a large stone marking a burial place.

_____

_____

12. To **evince** pleasure is to show that one is feeling it.

_____

_____

13. To **enshrine** a deed is to honor it as something worthy of remembering.

_____

_____

14. To **patronize** someone is to fail to show respect for that person.

_____

_____

15. To **refute** something is to accept it on another person's behalf.

_____

_____

If the word (or a form of the word) in bold fits in a sentence in the group following it, write the word in the blank space. If the word does not fit, leave the space empty. There may be more than one correct answer.

1. **evince**

    (a) Fernando _____ no sign that he had heard my whispered remark.

    (b) Her revised proposal _____ a change of attitude on her part.

    (c) My repeated attempts at conversation _____ no response from my partner.

2. **quirk**

    (a) It was a _____ of his not to step on the cracks between the tiles.

    (b) Gail couldn't hide the _____ on her face after fooling us so completely.

    (c) By a _____ of nature, lightning did strike twice in the same spot.

3. **patronize**

    (a) When China resumed nuclear testing, we refused to _____ Chinese goods.

    (b) We _____ this fruit and vegetable store because we have known the owner for many years.

    (c) "I'm just as adept at this as you are, so don't _____ me," asserted Luisa.

4. **mundane**

    (a) His thoughts are on a higher plane and he does not dwell on _____ matters.

    (b) Being a test pilot is hardly a _____ occupation.

    (c) The monks spend part of each day on such _____ tasks as pulling up weeds.

5. **devise**

    (a) Is it possible to _____ a test to measure a person's artistic ability?

    (b) This _____ detects carbon monoxide poisoning.

    (c) The author has managed to _____ a most ingenious plot for her new novel.

6. **sanction**

    (a) By remaining silent, you appear to _____ teenage drinking.

    (b) Libya sought ways to get around the _____ against its export of oil.

    (c) Although these customs seem foolish, they have the _____ of long tradition.

bogus
demise
devise
enshrine
evince
irrevocable
martial
memorabilia
mundane
patronize
querulous
quirk
refute
sanction
tome

7. **martial**

    (a) The Spartans of ancient Greece were a _____ people.

    (b) A local Olympic gold medal winner was chosen as the parade _____ .

    (c) The people's _____ spirit was wearing thin after four years of war.

8. **querulous**

    (a) In a _____ voice, he scolded her for not visiting him more often.

    (b) The speaker reminded us that these are _____ times for our country.

    (c) The poet writes of the _____ boredom of a child with too many toys.

20c Word Study

Fill in the missing word in each sentence. Then write a brief definition of the word. The number in parentheses shows the lesson in which the word appears.

1. The prefix *ad-* (to) combines with the Latin verb *haerere* (to stick) to form the word

    _____ (18).

    Definition: _____

2. The prefix *re-* (back) combines with the Latin verb *scindere* (to split) to form the word

    _____ (19).

    Definition: _____

3. The Latin *multus* (many) gives us the word _____ (19).

    Definition: _____

4. The prefixes *ir-* (not) and *re-* (back) combine with the Latin verb *vocare* (to call) to form

    the word _____ (20).

    Definition: _____

5. The Latin *suavis* (sweet; delightful) gives us the word _____ (19).

    Definition: _____

6. The Latin *nomen* (name) gives us the word _____ (17).

    Definition: _____

7. The prefix *extra-* (beyond) combines with the Latin verb *vagari* (to wander) to form the word _____ (18).

   Definition: _____

8. The Latin *tenere* (to hold) gives us the word _____ (18).

   Definition: _____

9. The Latin *queri* (to complain) gives us the word _____ (20).

   Definition: _____

10. The prefix *col-* (together) combines with the Latin *ludere* (to play) to form the word _____ (19).

    Definition: _____

20D ▷ Images of Words

Circle the letter of each sentence that suggests the numbered bold vocabulary word. In each group, you may circle more than one letter or none at all.

1. **tome**
   (a) Kimy took the book from the back pocket of her jeans and began reading.
   (b) Cynthia dropped Volume 3 on her foot, almost breaking her big toe.
   (c) The book was unreadable but made a good doorstop.

2. **enshrine**
   (a) The names of all those who made a contribution are kept in a book of remembrance.
   (b) The United States Constitution is memorialized in a special display case in Washington, D.C.
   (c) Sammy keeps his collection of sea shells in a keepsake box.

3. **patronize**
   (a) The Blue Parrot is my favorite restaurant in town.
   (b) Emily Hurst set up a fund to help struggling artists.
   (c) I enjoyed my first visit to Seattle.

4. **refute**
   (a) He didn't expect that I'd score any points, but I made two field goals.
   (b) After Magellan had sailed around the world, most people no longer thought it was flat.
   (c) I was offered a job as a law clerk, but I turned it down.

bogus
demise
devise
enshrine
evince
irrevocable
martial
memorabilia
mundane
patronize
querulous
quirk
refute
sanction
tome

5. **bogus**

   (a) News reporter Elizabeth Cochran Seaman wrote under the pseudonym Nellie Bly.

   (b) I want you to make an exact copy of this document.

   (c) I became suspicious when the customer handed me a three-dollar bill.

6. **sanction**

   (a) It's no longer illegal to park on this city's streets overnight.

   (b) NATO members are debating whether or not to expand the organization.

   (c) The area was divided into four parts of roughly equal size.

7. **memorabilia**

   (a) She writes herself notes so she won't forget what she has to do.

   (b) Reggie can tell you the names of every major league player since 1900.

   (c) Looking through these old postcards brought back happy memories.

8. **demise**

   (a) Juanita finished the last page and closed the book with a sigh of relief.

   (b) Critics had been predicting the end of the British film industry for years.

   (c) The company is expected to shut down within three to four weeks.

9. **irrevocable**

   (a) There is no one who could take Marion's place in our book group.

   (b) It is hard to play against a team with a sixteen-game winning streak.

   (c) Once Grandpa makes a decision there's no changing it.

10. **evince**

   (a) Joe might be willing to buy the car if we can agree on a price.

   (b) A look of fear came into her eyes when she saw the tornado approaching.

   (c) The headline said "Record High Temperatures Set."

Read the passage. Then answer the questions that follow it.

Who Invented Baseball?

Popular legend tells us that baseball was invented in 1839 by Abner Doubleday. When Doubleday died on January 26, 1893, he might reasonably have been expected to be remembered, if at all, for his **martial** exploits as a Union general during the Civil War or as the author of two substantial **tomes** on that conflict, written in the years of his retirement. But in a curious **quirk** of history, Abner Doubleday is today remembered by most people for neither of these accomplishments. He is famous for having invented baseball.

The story goes that one day in the summer of 1839, Doubleday, then a youth living in Cooperstown, New York, **devised** the rules of the game that grew to be America's national pastime. The truth is almost certainly quite different. At that time, Doubleday was spending his second year as a cadet at West Point. And although he attended school in Cooperstown, there is no reliable evidence that he was there that particular year. Nor is there any evidence that he ever **evinced** the slightest interest in baseball. How, then, did his name become **irrevocably** associated with the game?

The formation of the National League in 1876 began the era of Major League Baseball. The addition of the American League in 1901 led to the first World Series two years later. Interest in the game soared, and fans **patronized** the game in ever-increasing numbers. It was natural that people began to wonder about its origins, and in 1905 baseball's ruling commission **sanctioned** the creation of a seven-member panel to inquire into the matter.

Among the many pieces of "evidence" the panel received was a letter from a retired mining engineer named Abner Graves. He claimed that at Cooperstown in 1839 Doubleday showed him a diagram for the game and explained its rules. The claim was almost certainly **bogus,** but that did not trouble the panel. Doubleday was a genuine American hero, just the sort of person needed to fill the role assigned to him. Furthermore, his **demise,** ten years before, made it impossible for him to **refute** the story.

Although a few **querulous** voices were raised in dissent, they were drowned out in the general chorus of approval of the panel's findings. The contention that baseball had evolved from the ancient English game of rounders was deemed erroneous. Baseball, it could confidently be asserted, was a thoroughly American creation.

In 1939, to mark the occasion of baseball's one-hundredth birthday, the Baseball Hall of Fame was inaugurated. Located in Cooperstown, halfway between Schenectady and Utica, New York, it occupies the original site of the cow patch on which, according to legend, the very first game of baseball was played. Included in its collection of baseball **memorabilia** is a scuffed and misshapen baseball. It was found in the attic of a nearby farmhouse in 1866 and the claim was made that it was the actual ball used in the historic 1839 game.

bogus
demise
devise
enshrine
evince
irrevocable
martial
memorabilia
mundane
patronize
querulous
quirk
refute
sanction
tome

Abner Doubleday almost certainly had nothing to do with the invention of baseball. The game did not have its birthplace in Cooperstown, and the ball **enshrined** in its Hall of Fame is highly unlikely to have had anything to do with the game's origins. But these considerations are all irrelevant. **Mundane** facts have little appeal, but myths, especially those with heroes, exert a powerful pull on the imagination. That is why the story of Abner Doubleday endures.

▶ **Answer each question in the form of a sentence. If a question does not contain a word from the lesson, use one in your answer. Use each word only once.**

1. Why might the Abner Doubleday myth be **enshrined** in the hearts of baseball fans?

   _____

   _____

2. How did the public respond to the panel's findings?

   _____

   _____

3. What kind of evidence could have challenged the claim that Doubleday invented baseball?

   _____

   _____

4. Why wasn't Greaves's testimony **refuted** by the panel?

   _____

   _____

5. When did fans start **patronizing** baseball games?

   _____

   _____

6. What kinds of **memorabilia** do you suppose are housed in the National Baseball Hall of Fame?

   _____

   _____

7. Why might Doubleday find fault with the way he is remembered?

   _____

   _____

8. How might Doubleday be more accurately remembered?

   _____

   _____

9. Why do you think **mundane** facts have little appeal?

_____

_____

10. Why is it a **quirk** of history that Doubleday is today remembered for having invented baseball?

_____

_____

FUN & FASCINATING FACTS

Several planets in our solar system have the names of ancient Roman gods. Some words that indicate particular human characteristics are derived from these names. For example, Jupiter, also called Jove, was the supreme deity of the Romans and is the name of the fifth planet from the sun, which is also the largest. A *jovial* person is believed to be under its influence, as indicated by this person's cheerful disposition.

The messenger of the gods was Mercury, the name of the planet closest to the sun. A *mercurial* person has the qualities of swiftness and cleverness associated with this god.

The fourth planet, lying between Earth and Jupiter, is Mars, named after the Roman god of war. A person showing a **martial** spirit is one ready to fight, one who exhibits the qualities of a warrior.

bogus

demise

devise

enshrine

evince

irrevocable

martial

memorabilia

mundane

patronize

querulous

quirk

refute

sanction

tome

Crossword Puzzle Solve the crossword puzzle by studying the clues and filling in the answer boxes. Clues followed by a number are definitions of words in Lessons 17 through 20. The number gives the word list in which the answer to the clue appears.

Clues Across

3. Capable of being defended or believed (18)
7. Often relating to ordinary, everyday matters (20)
9. The end of existence or activity; death (20)
10. To bring up for discussion (18)
11. Dirty or disgusting (19)
14. To stick to (18)
17. To defeat or overcome (18)
19. Smoothly polite; blandly pleasing (19)
20. Opposite of "take"
22. Funny in a crude way (17)
24. Abbreviation for "Incorporated"
26. To cherish as precious or sacred (20)
27. A demonstration of strong approval or praise (18)
28. To charge with a crime (19)

Clues Down

1. A peculiar or eccentric mannerism (20)
2. Approval or permission from an authority (20)
3. A book, especially one that is large (20)
4. The highest point of something (19)
5. Famous movie dog
6. Expressing sorrow; mournful (18)
8. An absurd or ridiculous event or situation (17)
9. An ardent follower, supporter, or enthusiast (18)
12. A yellow fruit
13. A distorted example or imitation (19)
15. Blood _____ (a breed of dog)
16. To do away with; to cancel (19)
18. Any disease that damages plants (17)
20. To gather bit by bit (17)
21. A cutting from a plant used to produce new growth (19)
23. Water _____ (an aquatic plant)
25. To mention for praise (17)

Pronunciation Key

Symbol	Key Words	Symbol	Key Words
a	cat	b	bed
ā	ape	d	dog
ä	cot, car	f	fall
â	bear	g	get
		h	help
e	ten, berry	j	jump
ē	me	k	kiss, call
		l	leg, bottle
i	fit	m	meat
ī	ice, fire	n	nose, kitten
		p	put
ō	go	r	red
ô	fall, for	s	see
oi	oil	t	top
ၹ	look, pull	v	vat
o͞o	tool, rule	w	wish
ou	out, crowd	y	yard
		z	zebra
u	up		
ʉ	fur, shirt	ch	chin, arch
		ŋ	ring, drink
ə	a in ago	sh	she, push
	e in agent	th	thin, truth
	i in pencil	*th*	then, father
	o in atom	zh	measure
	u in circus		
´	hospital (häs´ pit'l)		

A stress mark ´ is placed after a syllable that gets a primary stress, as in **vocabulary** (vō kab´ yə ler ē).